MznLnx

Missing Links Exam Preps

Exam Prep for

Microeconomic Theory

Mas-Colell, Whinston, & Green, 1st Edition

The MznLnx Exam Prep is your link from the texbook and lecture to your exams.
The MznLnx Exam Preps are unauthorized and comprehensive reviews of your textbooks.

All material provided by MznLnx and Rico Publications (c) 2010
Textbook publishers and textbook authors do not particpate in or contribute to these reviews.

MznLnx

Rico
Publications

Exam Prep for Microeconomic Theory
1st Edition
Mas-Colell, Whinston, & Green

Publisher: Raymond Houge
Assistant Editor: Michael Rouger
Text and Cover Designer: Lisa Buckner
Marketing Manager: Sara Swagger
Project Manager, Editorial Production: Jerry Emerson
Art Director: Vernon Lowerui

Product Manager: Dave Mason
Editorial Assitant: Rachel Guzmanji
Pedagogy: Debra Long
Cover Image: Jim Reed/Getty Images
Text and Cover Printer: City Printing, Inc.
Compositor: Media Mix, Inc.

(c) 2010 Rico Publications

ALL RIGHTS RESERVED. No part of this work covered by the copyright may be reproduced or used in any form or by an means--graphic, electronic, or mechanical, including photocopying, recording, taping, Web distribution, information storage, and retrieval systems, or in any other manner--without the written permission of the publisher.

Printed in the United States
ISBN:

For more information about our products, contact us at:
Dave.Mason@RicoPublications.com

For permission to use material from this text or product, submit a request online to:
Dave.Mason@RicoPublications.com

Contents

CHAPTER 1
Preference and Choice — 1

CHAPTER 2
Consumer Choice — 4

CHAPTER 3
Classical Demand Theory — 9

CHAPTER 4
Aggregate Demand — 18

CHAPTER 5
Production — 23

CHAPTER 6
Choice Under Uncertainty — 28

CHAPTER 7
Basic Elements of Noncooperative Games — 34

CHAPTER 8
Simultaneous-Move Games — 38

CHAPTER 9
Dynamic Games — 42

CHAPTER 10
Competitive Markets — 48

CHAPTER 11
Externalities and Public Goods — 57

CHAPTER 12
Market Power — 62

CHAPTER 13
Adverse Selection, Signaling, and Screening — 71

CHAPTER 14
The Principal-Agent Problem — 77

CHAPTER 15
General Equilibrium Theory: Some Examples — 80

CHAPTER 16
Equilibrium and Its Basic Welfare Properties — 87

CHAPTER 17
The Positive Theory of Equilibrium — 95

CHAPTER 18
Some Foundations for Competitive Equilibria — 101

CHAPTER 19
General Equilibrium Under Uncertainty — 108

CHAPTER 20
Equilibrium and Time — 116

Contents (Cont.)

CHAPTER 21
Social Choice Theory — 126

CHAPTER 22
Elements of Welfare Economics and Axiomatic Bargaining — 129

CHAPTER 23
Incentives and Mechanism Design — 135

ANSWER KEY — 146

TO THE STUDENT

COMPREHENSIVE

The *MznLnx* Exam Prep series is designed to help you pass your exams. Editors at MznLnx review your textbooks and then prepare these practice exams to help you master the textbook material. Unlike study guides, workbooks, and practice tests provided by the texbook publisher and textbook authors, *MznLnx* gives you **all** of the material in each chapter in exam form, not just samples, so you can be sure to nail your exam.

MECHANICAL

The MznLnx Exam Prep series creates exams that will help you learn the subject matter as well as test you on your understanding. Each question is designed to help you master the concept. Just working through the exams, you gain an understanding of the subject--its a simple mechanical process that produces success.

INTEGRATED STUDY GUIDE AND REVIEW

MznLnx is not just a set of exams designed to test you, its also a comprehensive review of the subject content. Each exam question is also a review of the concept, making sure that you will get the answer correct without having to go to other sources of material. You learn as you go! Its the easiest way to pass an exam.

HUMOR

Studying can be tedious and dry. MznLnx's instructional design includes moderate humor within the exam questions on occassion, to break the tedium and revitalize the brain

Chapter 1. Preference and Choice

1. _____ theory, pioneered by American economist Paul Samuelson, is a method by which it is possible to discern the best possible option on the basis of consumer behavior. Essentially, this means that the preferences of consumers can be revealed by their purchasing habits. _____ theory came about because the theories of consumer demand were based on a diminishing marginal rate of substitution (MRS.)
   a. Joint demand
   b. Marginal rate of substitution
   c. Rational addiction
   d. Revealed preference

2. _____ theory is a branch of theoretical economics. It seeks to explain the behavior of supply, demand and prices in a whole economy with several or many markets. It is often assumed that agents are price takers and in that setting two common notions of equilibrium exist: Walrasian (or competitive) equilibrium, and its generalization; a price equilibrium with transfers.
   a. General equilibrium
   b. New Keynesian economics
   c. Rational choice theory
   d. Human capital

3. In economics, _____ is a measure of the relative satisfaction from consumption of various goods and services. Given this measure, one may speak meaningfully of increasing or decreasing _____, and thereby explain economic behavior in terms of attempts to increase one's _____. For illustrative purposes, changes in _____ are sometimes expressed in units called utils.
   a. Expected utility hypothesis
   b. Utility
   c. Ordinal utility
   d. Utility function

4. While preferences are the conventional foundation of microeconomics, it is often convenient to represent preferences with a _____ and reason indirectly about preferences with _____s. Let X be the consumption set, the set of all mutually-exclusive packages the consumer could conceivably consume (such as an indifference curve map without the indifference curves.) The consumer's _____ $u : X \to \mathbf{R}$ ranks each package in the consumption set.
   a. Utility
   b. Ordinal utility
   c. Expected utility hypothesis
   d. Utility function

5. The _____ is the apparent contradiction that although water is on the whole more useful, in terms of survival, than diamonds, diamonds command a higher price in the market. The economist Adam Smith is often considered to be the classic presenter of this paradox. Nicolaus Copernicus, John Locke, John Law and others had previously tried to explain the disparity.
   a. Paradox of value
   b. 100-year flood
   c. 130-30 fund
   d. St. Petersburg paradox

Chapter 1. Preference and Choice

6. A _____ is:

- Rewrite _____, in generative grammar and computer science
- Standardization, a formal and widely-accepted statement, fact, definition, or qualification
- Operation, a determinate _____ for performing a mathematical operation and obtaining a certain result (Mathematics, Logic)
    - Unary operation
    - Binary operation
- _____ of inference, a function from sets of formulae to formulae (Mathematics, Logic)
- _____ of thumb, principle with broad application that is not intended to be strictly accurate or reliable for every situation. Also often simply referred to as a _____
- Moral, an atomic element of a moral code for guiding choices in human behavior
- Heuristic, a quantized '_____' which shows a tendency or probability for successful function
- A regulation, as in sports
- A Production _____, as in computer science
- Procedural law, a _____ set governing the application of laws to cases
    - A law, which may informally be called a '_____'
    - A court ruling, a decision by a court
- In the U.S. Government, a regulation mandated by Congress, but written or expanded upon by the Executive Branch.
- Norm (sociology), an informal but widely accepted _____, concept, truth, definition, or qualification (social norms, legal norms, coding norms)
- Norm (philosophy), a kind of sentence or a reason to act, feel or believe
- 'Rulership' is the concept of governance by a government:
    - Military _____, governance by a military body
    - Monastic _____, a collection of precepts that guides the life of monks or nuns in a religious order where the superior holds the place of Christ
- Slide _____

- '_____,' a song by Ayumi Hamasaki
- '_____,' a song by rapper Nas
- '_____s,' an album by the band The Whitest Boy Alive
- _____s: Pyaar Ka Superhit Formula, a 2003 Bollywood film
- ruler, an instrument for measuring lengths
- _____, a component of an astrolabe, circumferator or similar instrument
- The _____s, a bestselling self-help book
- _____ Project (Run Up-to-date Linux Everywhere), a project that aims to use up-to-date Linux software on old PCs
- _____ engine, a software system that helps managing business _____s
- Ja _____, a hip hop artist
    - R.U.L.E., a 2005 greatest hits album by rapper Ja _____
- '_____s,' a KMFDM song

a. Technocracy
b. Demand
c. Procter ' Gamble
d. Rule

7. A _____ includes all possible consumption bundles that someone can afford given the prices of goods and the person's income level. The _____ is bounded above by the budget line.
   a. 130-30 fund
   b. Budget surplus
   c. Budget set
   d. 100-year flood

Chapter 2. Consumer Choice

1. _____ is a broad label that refers to any individuals or households that use goods and services generated within the economy. The concept of a _____ is used in different contexts, so that the usage and significance of the term may vary.

Typically when business people and economists talk of _____s they are talking about person as _____, an aggregated commodity item with little individuality other than that expressed in the buy/not-buy decision.

   a. Consumer
   c. 1921 recession
   b. 100-year flood
   d. 130-30 fund

2. Economics:

   - _____,the desire to own something and the ability to pay for it
   - _____ curve,a graphic representation of a _____ schedule
   - _____ deposit, the money in checking accounts
   - _____ pull theory,the theory that inflation occurs when _____ for goods and services exceeds existing supplies
   - _____ schedule,a table that lists the quantity of a good a person will buy it each different price
   - _____ side economics,the school of economics at believes government spending and tax cuts open economy by raising _____

   a. McKesson ' Robbins scandal
   c. Production
   b. Variability
   d. Demand

3. A _____ is something for which there is demand, but which is supplied without qualitative differentiation across a market. It is a product that is the same no matter who produces it, such as petroleum, notebook paper, or milk. In other words, copper is copper.
   a. Hard commodity
   c. Commodity
   b. Soft commodity
   d. 100-year flood

4. _____ is a common concept in economics, and gives rise to derived concepts such as consumer debt. Generally _____ is defined by opposition to production. But the precise definition can vary because different schools of economists define production quite differently.
   a. Cash or share options
   c. Federal Reserve Bank Notes
   b. Foreclosure data providers
   d. Consumption

5. In social choice theory, _____ is a property of social welfare functions in which all preferences of all voters are factored into the final ordering of societal choices. Intuitively, _____ is a common requirement for social choice functions, and is a condition for Arrow's impossibility theorem.

With _____, the social welfare function accounts for all preferences among all voters to yield a unique and complete ranking of societal choices.

a. ACEA agreement	b. Unrestricted domain
c. ACCRA Cost of Living Index	d. AD-IA Model

6. A _____ includes all possible consumption bundles that someone can afford given the prices of goods and the person's income level. The _____ is bounded above by the budget line.

a. Budget set	b. 130-30 fund
c. Budget surplus	d. 100-year flood

7. In economics, _____ is a measure of the relative satisfaction from consumption of various goods and services. Given this measure, one may speak meaningfully of increasing or decreasing _____, and thereby explain economic behavior in terms of attempts to increase one's _____. For illustrative purposes, changes in _____ are sometimes expressed in units called utils.

a. Utility function	b. Expected utility hypothesis
c. Ordinal utility	d. Utility

8. While preferences are the conventional foundation of microeconomics, it is often convenient to represent preferences with a _____ and reason indirectly about preferences with _____s. Let X be the consumption set, the set of all mutually-exclusive packages the consumer could conceivably consume (such as an indifference curve map without the indifference curves.) The consumer's _____ $u : X \to \mathbf{R}$ ranks each package in the consumption set.

a. Expected utility hypothesis	b. Utility
c. Utility function	d. Ordinal utility

9. In economics, _____ is the comparison of two different equilibrium states, before and after a change in some underlying exogenous parameter. As a study of statics it compares two different unchanging points, after they have changed. It does not study the motion towards equilibrium, nor the process of the change itself.

a. Comparative statics	b. Customer equity
c. Social surplus	d. Feasibility condition

10. The _____ is an economic term, referring to an increase in spending that accompanies an increase or perceived increase in wealth.

The effect would cause changes in the amounts and composition of consumer consumption caused by changes in consumer wealth. People should spend more when one of two things is true: when people actually are richer (by objective measurement, for example, a bonus or a pay raise at work, which would be an income effect), or when people perceive themselves to be 'richer' (for example, the assessed value of their home increases, or a stock they own has gone up in price recently.)

a. 100-year flood	b. Wealth condensation
c. Wealth effect	d. 130-30 fund

11. In economics and particularly in international trade, an _____ shows the quantity of one type of product that an agent will export ('offer') for each quantity of another type of product that it imports. The _____ was first derived by English economists Edgeworth and Marshall to help explain international trade.

The _____ is derived from the country's PPF.

a. ACCRA Cost of Living Index
b. ACEA agreement
c. AD-IA Model
d. Offer curve

12. _____ in economics and business is the result of an exchange and from that trade we assign a numerical monetary value to a good, service or asset. If Alice trades Bob 4 apples for an orange, the _____ of an orange is 4 apples. Inversely, the _____ of an apple is 1/4 oranges.
a. Price
b. Price book
c. Premium pricing
d. Price war

13. In economics and consumer theory, a _____ is one which people consume more of as price rises, violating the law of demand. In normal situations, as the price of such a good rises, the substitution effect causes people to purchase less of it and more of substitute goods. In the _____ situation, cheaper close substitutes are not available.
a. Pie method
b. Demerit good
c. Search good
d. Giffen good

14. A _____ is an object whose consumption increases the utility of the consumer, for which the quantity demanded exceeds the quantity supplied at zero price. _____s are usually modeled as having diminishing marginal utility. The first individual purchase has high utility; the second has less.
a. Merit good
b. Pie method
c. Composite good
d. Good

15. In economics, _____ is the ratio of the percent change in one variable to the percent change in another variable. It is a tool for measuring the responsiveness of a function to changes in parameters in a relative way. Commonly analyzed are _____ of substitution, price and wealth.
a. Elasticity of demand
b. Elasticity
c. ACEA agreement
d. ACCRA Cost of Living Index

16. Price _____ is defined as the measure of responsiveness in the quantity demanded for a commodity as a result of change in price of the same commodity. It is a measure of how consumers react to a change in price. In other words, it is percentage change in quantity demanded by the percentage change in price of the same commodity.
a. Elasticity of demand
b. ACEA agreement
c. Elasticity
d. ACCRA Cost of Living Index

17. _____ theory, pioneered by American economist Paul Samuelson, is a method by which it is possible to discern the best possible option on the basis of consumer behavior. Essentially, this means that the preferences of consumers can be revealed by their purchasing habits. _____ theory came about because the theories of consumer demand were based on a diminishing marginal rate of substitution (MRS.)
a. Joint demand
b. Rational addiction
c. Marginal rate of substitution
d. Revealed preference

18. In economics, the _____ is an economic law that states that consumers buy more of a good when its price decreases and less when its price increases.

There are certain goods which do not follow this law. These include Veblen and Giffen goods

a. Law of demand b. Georgism
c. Market failure d. Financial crisis

19. A _____ is:

- Rewrite _____, in generative grammar and computer science
- Standardization, a formal and widely-accepted statement, fact, definition, or qualification
- Operation, a determinate _____ for performing a mathematical operation and obtaining a certain result (Mathematics, Logic)
    - Unary operation
    - Binary operation
- _____ of inference, a function from sets of formulae to formulae (Mathematics, Logic)
- _____ of thumb, principle with broad application that is not intended to be strictly accurate or reliable for every situation. Also often simply referred to as a _____
- Moral, an atomic element of a moral code for guiding choices in human behavior
- Heuristic, a quantized '_____' which shows a tendency or probability for successful function
- A regulation, as in sports
- A Production _____, as in computer science
- Procedural law, a _____ set governing the application of laws to cases
    - A law, which may informally be called a '_____'
    - A court ruling, a decision by a court
- In the U.S. Government, a regulation mandated by Congress, but written or expanded upon by the Executive Branch.
- Norm (sociology), an informal but widely accepted _____, concept, truth, definition, or qualification (social norms, legal norms, coding norms)
- Norm (philosophy), a kind of sentence or a reason to act, feel or believe
- 'Rulership' is the concept of governance by a government:
    - Military _____, governance by a military body
    - Monastic _____, a collection of precepts that guides the life of monks or nuns in a religious order where the superior holds the place of Christ
- Slide _____

- '_____,' a song by Ayumi Hamasaki
- '_____,' a song by rapper Nas
- '_____s,' an album by the band The Whitest Boy Alive
- _____s: Pyaar Ka Superhit Formula, a 2003 Bollywood film
- ruler, an instrument for measuring lengths
- _____, a component of an astrolabe, circumferator or similar instrument
- The _____s, a bestselling self-help book
- _____ Project (Run Up-to-date Linux Everywhere), a project that aims to use up-to-date Linux software on old PCs
- _____ engine, a software system that helps managing business _____s
- Ja _____, a hip hop artist
    - R.U.L.E., a 2005 greatest hits album by rapper Ja _____
- '_____s,' a KMFDM song

a. Rule
c. Demand
b. Procter ' Gamble
d. Technocracy

Chapter 3. Classical Demand Theory

1. In finance, _____ is a measure of the sensitivity of the duration of a bond to changes in interest rates. There is an inverse relationship between _____ and sensitivity - in general, the higher the _____ less sensitive the bond price is to interest rate shifts, the lower the _____, the more sensitive it is.

Duration is a linear measure or 1st derivative of how the price of a bond changes in response to interest rate changes.

   a. Convexity
   b. Russian financial crisis
   c. Rule
   d. Technocracy

2. In economics, a consumer's preferences are said to be _____ if adding more of a good to the consumer's consumption bundle does not make him/her worse off. They are said to be strongly monotone if adding more of a good to the consumer's consumption bundle makes him/her strictly better off.

Note that in cases where the good in question is a 'bad' (i.e.undersirable) it is a simple matter to redefine the notion of the good as its negative.

   a. Compound Interest Treasury Notes
   b. Weakly monotone
   c. Bank rescue package
   d. Basis of futures

3. In economics and consumer theory, _____ functions are linear in one argument, generally the numeraire. Formally, for example, such a utility function could be written U(x,y) = u(x) + by, where b is a positive constant. Then if u'(x) > 0 and u''(x) < 0, the indifference curves are parallel.
   a. Gross value added
   b. False billing
   c. Direct Market Access
   d. Quasilinear utility

4. A _____ is something for which there is demand, but which is supplied without qualitative differentiation across a market. It is a product that is the same no matter who produces it, such as petroleum, notebook paper, or milk. In other words, copper is copper.
   a. Hard commodity
   b. 100-year flood
   c. Soft commodity
   d. Commodity

5. In economics, _____ is a measure of the relative satisfaction from consumption of various goods and services. Given this measure, one may speak meaningfully of increasing or decreasing _____, and thereby explain economic behavior in terms of attempts to increase one's _____. For illustrative purposes, changes in _____ are sometimes expressed in units called utils.
   a. Expected utility hypothesis
   b. Utility function
   c. Ordinal utility
   d. Utility

6. While preferences are the conventional foundation of microeconomics, it is often convenient to represent preferences with a _____ and reason indirectly about preferences with _____s. Let X be the consumption set, the set of all mutually-exclusive packages the consumer could conceivably consume (such as an indifference curve map without the indifference curves.) The consumer's _____ $u : X \to \mathbf{R}$ ranks each package in the consumption set.
   a. Ordinal utility
   b. Utility
   c. Expected utility hypothesis
   d. Utility function

Chapter 3. Classical Demand Theory

7. In microeconomics, the _____ is the problem consumers face: 'how should I spend my money in order to maximize my utility?'

Suppose their consumption set, or the enumeration of all possible consumption bundles that could be selected if there are no budget constraints has L commodities and is limited to positive amounts of consumption of each

$$x \in \mathbf{R}_+^L.$$

Suppose also that the prices (p) of the L commodities are positive

$$p \in \mathbf{R}_+^L,$$

and the consumer's wealth is w, then the set of all affordable packages, the budget set, is

$$B(p, w) = \{x \in \mathbf{R}_+^L : \langle p, x \rangle \leq w\},$$

where $\langle p, x \rangle$ is the inner product of p and x, or the total cost of consuming x of the products at price level p. The consumer would like to buy the best package of commodities it can afford. Suppose that the consumer's utility function (u) is a real valued function with domain of the commodity bundles, or

$$u : \mathbf{R}_+^L \to \mathbf{R}.$$

Then the consumer's optimal choices x(p, w) are the utility maximizing bundle that is in the budget set, or

$$x(p, w) = \mathrm{argmax}_{x^* \in B(p,w)} u(x^*).$$

a. Utility maximization problem
b. Income elasticity of demand
c. Expenditure minimization problem
d. Induced consumption

8. In microeconomics, a consumer's _____ specifies what the consumer would buy in each price and wealth situation, assuming it perfectly solves the utility maximization problem. Marshallian demand is sometimes called Walrasian demand or uncompensated demand function instead, because the original Marshallian analysis ignored wealth effects.

According to the utility maximization problem, there are L commodities with prices p.

a. Marshallian demand function
b. Precautionary demand
c. Kinked demand curve
d. Marginal demand

Chapter 3. Classical Demand Theory

9. Economics:

   - _____ ,the desire to own something and the ability to pay for it
   - _____ curve, a graphic representation of a _____ schedule
   - _____ deposit, the money in checking accounts
   - _____ pull theory, the theory that inflation occurs when _____ for goods and services exceeds existing supplies
   - _____ schedule, a table that lists the quantity of a good a person will buy it each different price
   - _____ side economics, the school of economics at believes government spending and tax cuts open economy by raising _____

   a. Variability
   c. Production
   b. McKesson ' Robbins scandal
   d. Demand

10. In mathematical optimization, the method of _____s provides a strategy for finding the maximum/minimum of a function subject to constraints.

For example, consider the optimization problem

maximize $f(x, y)$
subject to $g(x, y) = c$.

We introduce a new variable (λ) called a _____, and study the Lagrange function defined by

$$\Lambda(x, y, \lambda) = f(x, y) + \lambda\Big(g(x, y) - c\Big).$$

(λ may be either added or subtracted.) If (x,y)â‰ is a maximum for the original constrained problem, then there exists a λ such that (x,y,λ)â‰ is a stationary point for the Lagrange function (stationary points are those points where the partial derivatives of Λ are zero.)

   a. Radfar ratio
   c. 100-year flood
   b. 130-30 fund
   d. Lagrange multiplier

11. In economics, the _____ is the rate at which a consumer is ready to give up one good in exchange for another good while maintaining the same level of satisfaction.

Under the standard assumption of neoclassical economics that goods and services are continuously divisible, the marginal rates of substitution will be the same regardless of the direction of exchange, and will correspond to the slope of an indifference curve (more precisely, to the slope multiplied by -1) passing through the consumption bundle in question, at that point: mathematically, it is the implicit derivative. MRS of Y for X is the amount of Y for which a consumer is willing to exchange for X locally.

a. Marginal rate of substitution
b. Supply and demand
c. Demand vacuum
d. Quality bias

12. In economics, the _____ functional form of production functions is widely used to represent the relationship of an output to inputs. It was proposed by Knut Wicksell (1851-1926), and tested against statistical evidence by Charles Cobb and Paul Douglas in 1900-1928.

For production, the function is

$$Y = AL^{\alpha}K^{\beta},$$

where:

- Y = total production (the monetary value of all goods produced in a year)
- L = labor input
- K = capital input
- A = total factor productivity
- α and β are the output elasticities of labor and capital, respectively. These values are constants determined by available technology.

Output elasticity measures the responsiveness of output to a change in levels of either labor or capital used in production, ceteris paribus. For example if α = 0.15, a 1% increase in labor would lead to approximately a 0.15% increase in output.

a. Demand-pull theory
b. Growth accounting
c. Social savings
d. Cobb-Douglas

13. In economics, the _____ of a good or of a service is the utility of the specific use to which an agent would put a given increase in that good or service, or of the specific use that would be abandoned in response to a given decrease. In other words, _____ is the utility of the marginal use -- which, on the assumption of economic rationality, would be the least urgent use of the good or service, from the best feasible combination of actions in which its use is included. Under the mainstream assumptions, the _____ of a good or service is the posited quantified change in utility obtained by increasing or by decreasing use of that good or service.

a. 1921 recession
b. 130-30 fund
c. Marginal utility
d. 100-year flood

14. In microeconomics, the _____ describes the minimum amount of money an individual needs to achieve some level of utility, given a utility function and prices.

Formally, if there is a utility function u that describes preferences over L commodities, the _____

$$e(p, u^*) : \mathbf{R}^L_+ \times \mathbf{R} \to \mathbf{R}$$

says what amount of money is needed to achieve a utility u * if prices are set by p. This function is defined by

$$e(p, u^*) = \min_{x \in \geq(u^*)} p \cdot x$$

where

$$\geq (u^*) = \{x \in \mathbf{R}^L_+ : u(x) \geq u^*\}$$

is the set of all packages that give utility at least as good as u *.

a. Expenditure minimization problem
b. Expenditure function
c. Income elasticity of demand
d. Indifference curve

15. In economics, the _____ is an economic law that states that consumers buy more of a good when its price decreases and less when its price increases.

There are certain goods which do not follow this law. These include Veblen and Giffen goods

a. Georgism
b. Law of demand
c. Market failure
d. Financial crisis

16. The _____ is a basic theorem used to solve maximization problems in microeconomics. It may be used to prove Hotelling's lemma, Shephard's lemma, and Roy's identity. The statement of the theorem is:

Consider an arbitrary maximization problem where the objective function (f) depends on some parameter (a):

$$M(a) = \max_x f(x, a)$$

where the function M(a) gives the maximized value of the objective function (f) as a function of the parameter (a.)

a. ACEA agreement
b. Envelope theorem
c. ACCRA Cost of Living Index
d. AD-IA Model

14 Chapter 3. Classical Demand Theory

17. A _____ is:

- Rewrite _____, in generative grammar and computer science
- Standardization, a formal and widely-accepted statement, fact, definition, or qualification
- Operation, a determinate _____ for performing a mathematical operation and obtaining a certain result (Mathematics, Logic)
    - Unary operation
    - Binary operation
- _____ of inference, a function from sets of formulae to formulae (Mathematics, Logic)
- _____ of thumb, principle with broad application that is not intended to be strictly accurate or reliable for every situation. Also often simply referred to as a _____
- Moral, an atomic element of a moral code for guiding choices in human behavior
- Heuristic, a quantized '_____' which shows a tendency or probability for successful function
- A regulation, as in sports
- A Production _____, as in computer science
- Procedural law, a _____ set governing the application of laws to cases
    - A law, which may informally be called a '_____'
    - A court ruling, a decision by a court
- In the U.S. Government, a regulation mandated by Congress, but written or expanded upon by the Executive Branch.
- Norm (sociology), an informal but widely accepted _____, concept, truth, definition, or qualification (social norms, legal norms, coding norms)
- Norm (philosophy), a kind of sentence or a reason to act, feel or believe
- 'Rulership' is the concept of governance by a government:
    - Military _____, governance by a military body
    - Monastic _____, a collection of precepts that guides the life of monks or nuns in a religious order where the superior holds the place of Christ
- Slide _____

- '_____,' a song by Ayumi Hamasaki
- '_____,' a song by rapper Nas
- '_____s,' an album by the band The Whitest Boy Alive
- _____s: Pyaar Ka Superhit Formula, a 2003 Bollywood film
- ruler, an instrument for measuring lengths
- _____, a component of an astrolabe, circumferator or similar instrument
- The _____s, a bestselling self-help book
- _____ Project (Run Up-to-date Linux Everywhere), a project that aims to use up-to-date Linux software on old PCs
- _____ engine, a software system that helps managing business _____s
- Ja _____, a hip hop artist
    - R.U.L.E., a 2005 greatest hits album by rapper Ja _____
- '_____s,' a KMFDM song

a. Demand
c. Rule

b. Technocracy
d. Procter ' Gamble

Chapter 3. Classical Demand Theory

18. _____ in economics and business is the result of an exchange and from that trade we assign a numerical monetary value to a good, service or asset. If Alice trades Bob 4 apples for an orange, the _____ of an orange is 4 apples. Inversely, the _____ of an apple is 1/4 oranges.

a. Premium pricing
b. Price war
c. Price
d. Price book

19. In microeconomics, a consumer's _____ is the demand of a consumer over a bundle of goods that minimizes their expenditure while delivering a fixed level of utility. The function is named after John Hicks.

Mathematically,

$$h(p, \bar{u}) = \arg\min_x \sum_i p_i x_i$$
$$\text{such that } u(x) > \bar{u}$$

where h is the _____, or commodity bundle demanded, at price level p and utility level $\bar{u}$.

a. Kinked demand curve
b. Precautionary demand
c. Kinked demand
d. Hicksian demand function

20. The _____ in economics relates changes in Marshallian demand to changes in Hicksian demand. It demonstrates that demand changes due to price changes are a result of two effects:

- a substitution effect, the result of a change in the exchange rate between two goods; and
- an income effect, the effect of price results in a change of the consumer's purchasing power.

Each element of the Slutsky matrix is given by

$$\frac{\partial x_i(p, w)}{\partial p_j} = \frac{\partial h_i(p, u)}{\partial p_j} - \frac{\partial x_i(p, w)}{\partial w} x_j(p, w),$$

where h(p,u) is the Hicksian demand and x(p,w) is the Marshallian demand, at price level p, wealth level w, and utility level u. The first term represents the substitution effect, and the second term represents the income effect.

The same equation can be rewritten in matrix form and is called the Slutsky matrix

$$D_p x(p, w) = D_p h(p, u) - D_w x(p, w) x(p, w)^\top,$$

where D_p is the derivative operator with respect to price and D_w is the derivative operator with respect to wealth.

a. Simultaneous equations
b. 100-year flood
c. 130-30 fund
d. Slutsky equation

Chapter 3. Classical Demand Theory

21. In economics, the _____ can be defined as the graph depicting the relationship between the price of a certain commodity, and the amount of it that consumers are willing and able to purchase at that given price. It is a graphic representation of a demand schedule. The _____ for all consumers together follows from the _____ of every individual consumer: the individual demands at each price are added together.
   a. Kuznets curve
   b. Wage curve
   c. Cost curve
   d. Demand curve

22. In economics, _____ is a measure of utility change introduced by John Hicks (1939.) '_____' refers to the amount of additional money an agent would need to reach its initial utility after a change in prices or the introduction of new products. _____ can be used to find the effect of a price change on an agent's net welfare.
   a. Deadweight loss
   b. Hidden Welfare State
   c. Compensating variation
   d. Gini coefficient

23. _____ is a measure of how much more money a consumer would pay before a price increase to avert the price increase. Because the meaning of 'equivalent' may be unclear, it is also called extortionary variation. John Hicks (1939) is attributed with introducing the concept of compensating and _____.
   a. International Social Security Association
   b. ACCRA Cost of Living Index
   c. Utility-possibility frontier
   d. Equivalent variation

24. _____ is a broad label that refers to any individuals or households that use goods and services generated within the economy. The concept of a _____ is used in different contexts, so that the usage and significance of the term may vary.

Typically when business people and economists talk of _____s they are talking about person as _____, an aggregated commodity item with little individuality other than that expressed in the buy/not-buy decision.

   a. 130-30 fund
   b. 1921 recession
   c. 100-year flood
   d. Consumer

25. The term surplus is used in economics for several related quantities. The _____ is the amount that consumers benefit by being able to purchase a product for a price that is less than they would be willing to pay. The producer surplus is the amount that producers benefit by selling at a market price mechanism that is higher than they would be willing to sell for.
   a. Necessity good
   b. Marginal rate of technical substitution
   c. Microeconomic reform
   d. Consumer surplus

26. In economics, a _____ is a loss of economic efficiency that can occur when equilibrium for a good or service is not Pareto optimal. In other words, either people who would have more marginal benefit than marginal cost are not buying the good or service, or people who would have more marginal cost than marginal benefit are buying the product.

Causes of _____ can include monopoly pricing, externalities, taxes or subsidies, and binding price ceilings or floors.

   a. Distributive efficiency
   b. Leapfrogging
   c. Contract curve
   d. Deadweight loss

Chapter 3. Classical Demand Theory

27. _____ theory, pioneered by American economist Paul Samuelson, is a method by which it is possible to discern the best possible option on the basis of consumer behavior. Essentially, this means that the preferences of consumers can be revealed by their purchasing habits. _____ theory came about because the theories of consumer demand were based on a diminishing marginal rate of substitution (MRS.)
   a. Revealed preference
   b. Rational addiction
   c. Marginal rate of substitution
   d. Joint demand

28. In economics, _____ is a property of some production functions and utility functions.

More precisely, it refers to a particular type of aggregator function which combines two or more types of consumption, or two or more types of productive inputs into an aggregate quantity. This aggregator function exhibits _____.

   a. Factors of production
   b. Product Pipeline
   c. Post-Fordism
   d. Constant elasticity of substitution

29. In economics, _____ is the ratio of the percent change in one variable to the percent change in another variable. It is a tool for measuring the responsiveness of a function to changes in parameters in a relative way. Commonly analyzed are _____ of substitution, price and wealth.
   a. ACCRA Cost of Living Index
   b. ACEA agreement
   c. Elasticity of demand
   d. Elasticity

30. _____ is the elasticity of the ratio of two inputs to a production (or utility) function with respect to the ratio of their marginal products (or utilities.) It measures the curvature of an isoquant.
   a. Indifference curve
   b. Elasticity of substitution
   c. Income elasticity of demand
   d. Indifference map

31. A _____ is an object whose consumption increases the utility of the consumer, for which the quantity demanded exceeds the quantity supplied at zero price. _____s are usually modeled as having diminishing marginal utility. The first individual purchase has high utility; the second has less.
   a. Composite good
   b. Pie method
   c. Merit good
   d. Good

Chapter 4. Aggregate Demand

1. In economics, _____ is the total demand for final goods and services in the economy (Y) at a given time and price level. It is the amount of goods and services in the economy that will be purchased at all possible price levels. This is the demand for the gross domestic product of a country when inventory levels are static.
   - a. Aggregate demand
   - b. Aggregation problem
   - c. Aggregate supply
   - d. Aggregate expenditure

2. Economics:

   - _____, the desire to own something and the ability to pay for it
   - _____ curve, a graphic representation of a _____ schedule
   - _____ deposit, the money in checking accounts
   - _____ pull theory, the theory that inflation occurs when _____ for goods and services exceeds existing supplies
   - _____ schedule, a table that lists the quantity of a good a person will buy it each different price
   - _____ side economics, the school of economics at believes government spending and tax cuts open economy by raising _____

   - a. Variability
   - b. McKesson ' Robbins scandal
   - c. Production
   - d. Demand

Chapter 4. Aggregate Demand 19

3. A _____ is:

- Rewrite _____, in generative grammar and computer science
- Standardization, a formal and widely-accepted statement, fact, definition, or qualification
- Operation, a determinate _____ for performing a mathematical operation and obtaining a certain result (Mathematics, Logic)
    - Unary operation
    - Binary operation
- _____ of inference, a function from sets of formulae to formulae (Mathematics, Logic)
- _____ of thumb, principle with broad application that is not intended to be strictly accurate or reliable for every situation. Also often simply referred to as a _____
- Moral, an atomic element of a moral code for guiding choices in human behavior
- Heuristic, a quantized '_____' which shows a tendency or probability for successful function
- A regulation, as in sports
- A Production _____, as in computer science
- Procedural law, a _____ set governing the application of laws to cases
    - A law, which may informally be called a '_____'
    - A court ruling, a decision by a court
- In the U.S. Government, a regulation mandated by Congress, but written or expanded upon by the Executive Branch.
- Norm (sociology), an informal but widely accepted _____, concept, truth, definition, or qualification (social norms, legal norms, coding norms)
- Norm (philosophy), a kind of sentence or a reason to act, feel or believe
- 'Rulership' is the concept of governance by a government:
    - Military _____, governance by a military body
    - Monastic _____, a collection of precepts that guides the life of monks or nuns in a religious order where the superior holds the place of Christ
- Slide _____

- '_____,' a song by Ayumi Hamasaki
- '_____,' a song by rapper Nas
- '_____s,' an album by the band The Whitest Boy Alive
- _____s: Pyaar Ka Superhit Formula, a 2003 Bollywood film
- ruler, an instrument for measuring lengths
- _____, a component of an astrolabe, circumferator or similar instrument
- The _____s, a bestselling self-help book
- _____ Project (Run Up-to-date Linux Everywhere), a project that aims to use up-to-date Linux software on old PCs
- _____ engine, a software system that helps managing business _____s
- Ja _____, a hip hop artist
    - R.U.L.E., a 2005 greatest hits album by rapper Ja _____
- '_____s,' a KMFDM song

a. Procter ' Gamble   b. Technocracy
c. Demand   d. Rule

Chapter 4. Aggregate Demand

4. _____ theory, pioneered by American economist Paul Samuelson, is a method by which it is possible to discern the best possible option on the basis of consumer behavior. Essentially, this means that the preferences of consumers can be revealed by their purchasing habits. _____ theory came about because the theories of consumer demand were based on a diminishing marginal rate of substitution (MRS.)

a. Joint demand
b. Rational addiction
c. Marginal rate of substitution
d. Revealed preference

5. In economics, the _____ is an economic law that states that consumers buy more of a good when its price decreases and less when its price increases.

There are certain goods which do not follow this law. These include Veblen and Giffen goods

a. Market failure
b. Financial crisis
c. Georgism
d. Law of demand

6. The _____ in economics relates changes in Marshallian demand to changes in Hicksian demand. It demonstrates that demand changes due to price changes are a result of two effects:

- a substitution effect, the result of a change in the exchange rate between two goods; and
- an income effect, the effect of price results in a change of the consumer's purchasing power.

Each element of the Slutsky matrix is given by

$$\frac{\partial x_i(p,w)}{\partial p_j} = \frac{\partial h_i(p,u)}{\partial p_j} - \frac{\partial x_i(p,w)}{\partial w} x_j(p,w),$$

where h(p,u) is the Hicksian demand and x(p,w) is the Marshallian demand, at price level p, wealth level w, and utility level u. The first term represents the substitution effect, and the second term represents the income effect.

The same equation can be rewritten in matrix form and is called the Slutsky matrix

$$D_p x(p,w) = D_p h(p,u) - D_w x(p,w) x(p,w)^\top,$$

where D_p is the derivative operator with respect to price and D_w is the derivative operator with respect to wealth.

a. Simultaneous equations
b. 100-year flood
c. 130-30 fund
d. Slutsky equation

7. _____ is a broad label that refers to any individuals or households that use goods and services generated within the economy. The concept of a _____ is used in different contexts, so that the usage and significance of the term may vary.

Chapter 4. Aggregate Demand

Typically when business people and economists talk of _____s they are talking about person as _____, an aggregated commodity item with little individuality other than that expressed in the buy/not-buy decision.

a. 100-year flood
c. 130-30 fund
b. Consumer
d. 1921 recession

8. In economics, _____ is a measure of the relative satisfaction from consumption of various goods and services. Given this measure, one may speak meaningfully of increasing or decreasing _____, and thereby explain economic behavior in terms of attempts to increase one's _____. For illustrative purposes, changes in _____ are sometimes expressed in units called utils.
a. Utility
c. Utility function
b. Ordinal utility
d. Expected utility hypothesis

9. While preferences are the conventional foundation of microeconomics, it is often convenient to represent preferences with a _____ and reason indirectly about preferences with _____s. Let X be the consumption set, the set of all mutually-exclusive packages the consumer could conceivably consume (such as an indifference curve map without the indifference curves.) The consumer's _____ $u : X \to \mathbf{R}$ ranks each package in the consumption set.
a. Utility
c. Expected utility hypothesis
b. Ordinal utility
d. Utility function

10. A _____ provision refers to any program which seeks to provide a minimum level of income, service or other support for many marginalized groups such as the poor, elderly, and disabled people. _____ programs are undertaken by governments as well as non-governmental organizations (NGOs.) _____ payments and services are typically provided at the expense of taxpayers generally, funded by benefactors, or by compulsory enrollment of the poor themselves.
a. 130-30 fund
c. 1921 recession
b. 100-year flood
d. Social welfare

11. In economics, a _____ is a real-valued function that ranks conceivable social states (alternative complete descriptions of the society) from lowest to highest. Inputs of the function include any variables considered to affect welfare of the society (Sen, 1970, p. 33.)
a. Gini coefficient
c. Contract curve
b. Frisch elasticity of labor supply
d. Social welfare function

12. In molecular kinetic theory in physics, a particle's _____ is a function of seven variables, f(x,y,z,t;v_x,v_y,v_z), which gives the number of particles per unit volume in phase space. It is the number of particles having approximately the velocity (v_x,v_y,v_z) near the place (x,y,z) and time (t). The usual normalization of the _____ is

$$n(x,y,z,t) = \int f \, dv_x \, dv_y \, dv_z$$

$$N(t) = \int n \, dx \, dy \, dz$$

Here, N is the total number of particles and n is the number density of particles - the number of particles per unit volume, or the density divided by the mass of individual particles.

a. 1921 recession
c. 100-year flood
b. Distribution function
d. 130-30 fund

13. In statistics, the _____ problem occurs when one considers a set of statistical inferences simultaneously. Errors in inference, including confidence intervals that fail to include their corresponding population parameters are more likely to occur when one considers the family as a whole. Several statistical techniques have been developed to prevent this from happening, allowing significance levels for single and _____ to be directly compared.

a. Familywise error rate
c. Multiple comparisons
b. False discovery rate
d. Hypotheses suggested by the data

Chapter 5. Production

1. In microeconomics, _____ is quite simply the conversion of inputs into outputs. It is an economic process that uses resources to create a good or service that is suitable for exchange. This can include manufacturing, storing, shipping, and packaging.
   a. Production
   b. Solved
   c. Red Guards
   d. MET

2. A _____ is the set of all possible input bundles that a firm can produce given its resources. Used as part of profit maximization calculations.
   a. 100-year flood
   b. 1921 recession
   c. Production set
   d. 130-30 fund

3. In economics, the _____ or the Technical Rate of Substitution (TRS) is the amount by which the quantity of one input has to be reduced ($-\Delta x_2$) when one extra unit of another input is used ($\Delta x_1 = 1$), so that output remains constant ($y = \bar{y}$.)

$$MRTS(x_1, x_2) = \frac{\Delta x_2}{\Delta x_1} = -\frac{MP_1}{MP_2}$$

where MP_1 and MP_2 are the marginal products of input 1 and input 2, respectively.

Along an isoquant, the MRTS shows the rate at which one input (e.g. capital or labor) may be substituted for another, while maintaining the same level of output.

   a. Producer surplus
   b. Pork cycle
   c. Marginal rate of technical substitution
   d. Household production function

4. The slope of the production-possibility frontier (PPF) at any given point is called the _____ It describes numerically the rate at which one good can be transformed into the other. It is also called the (marginal) 'opportunity cost' of a commodity, that is, it is the opportunity cost of X in terms of Y at the margin.
   a. Fordism
   b. Productivity
   c. Marginal rate of transformation
   d. Piece work

5. In economics, a _____ is a function that specifies the output of a firm, an industry, or an entire economy for all combinations of inputs. A meta-_____ compares the practice of the existing entities converting inputs X into output y to determine the most efficient practice _____ of the existing entities, whether the most efficient feasible practice production or the most efficient actual practice production. In either case, the maximum output of a technologically-determined production process is a mathematical function of input factors of production.
   a. Short-run
   b. Post-Fordism
   c. Production function
   d. Constant elasticity of substitution

6. In economics, the _____ functional form of production functions is widely used to represent the relationship of an output to inputs. It was proposed by Knut Wicksell (1851-1926), and tested against statistical evidence by Charles Cobb and Paul Douglas in 1900-1928.

Chapter 5. Production

For production, the function is

$$Y = AL^{\alpha}K^{\beta},$$

where:

- Y = total production (the monetary value of all goods produced in a year)
- L = labor input
- K = capital input
- A = total factor productivity
- α and β are the output elasticities of labor and capital, respectively. These values are constants determined by available technology.

Output elasticity measures the responsiveness of output to a change in levels of either labor or capital used in production, ceteris paribus. For example if α = 0.15, a 1% increase in labor would lead to approximately a 0.15% increase in output.

a. Growth accounting	b. Social savings
c. Demand-pull theory	d. Cobb-Douglas

7.   In economics and business decision-making, _____ are costs that cannot be recovered once they have been incurred. _____ are sometimes contrasted with variable costs, which are the costs that will change due to the proposed course of action, and prospective costs which are costs that will be incurred if an action is taken.

In traditional microeconomic theory, only variable costs are relevant to a decision.

a. Halo effect	b. Hyperbolic discounting
c. Sunk costs	d. Post-purchase rationalization

8.   In production, returns to scale refers to changes in output subsequent to a proportional change in all inputs (where all inputs increase by a constant factor.) If output increases by that same proportional change then there are _____ If output increases by less than that proportional change, there are decreasing returns to scale (DRS.)

a. Consumer sovereignty	b. Lexicographic preferences
c. Long term	d. Constant returns to scale

9.   In economics, _____ and economies of scale are related terms that describe what happens as the scale of production increases. They are different terms and should not be used interchangeably.

_____ refers to a technical property of production that examines changes in output subsequent to a proportional change in all inputs (where all inputs increase by a constant factor.)

a. Constant returns to scale	b. Necessity good
c. Customer equity	d. Returns to scale

Chapter 5. Production

10. In finance, _____ is a measure of the sensitivity of the duration of a bond to changes in interest rates. There is an inverse relationship between _____ and sensitivity - in general, the higher the _____ less sensitive the bond price is to interest rate shifts, the lower the _____, the more sensitive it is.

Duration is a linear measure or 1st derivative of how the price of a bond changes in response to interest rate changes.

a. Russian financial crisis
b. Rule
c. Convexity
d. Technocracy

11. _____ is a term used by economists to describe a condition in which firms can freely enter the market for an economic good by establishing production and beginning to sell the product.

_____ is implied by the perfect competition condition that there is an unlimited number of buyers and sellers in a market. In comparison to perfect competition, however, _____ is a condition often more applicable to real world conditions.

a. 130-30 fund
b. 1921 recession
c. 100-year flood
d. Free entry

12. In economics, _____ is the process by which a firm determines the price and output level that returns the greatest profit. There are several approaches to this problem. The total revenue--total cost method relies on the fact that profit equals revenue minus cost, and the marginal revenue--marginal cost method is based on the fact that total profit in a perfectly competitive market reaches its maximum point where marginal revenue equals marginal cost.

a. Profit margin
b. 100-year flood
c. Normal profit
d. Profit maximization

13. In economics, the _____ is the tendency of suppliers to offer more of a good at a higher price. The relationship between price and quantity supplied is usually a positive relationship. A rise in price is associated with a rise in quantity supplied.

a. Market failure
b. Mathematical economics
c. Heterodox economics
d. Law of supply

14. In economics, _____ defines the cost-minimizing level of an input required to produce a given level of output, for given costs (wages or rents) of various input factors. The conditional portion of this phrase refers to the fact that this function takes a given output as an argument, and is therefore conditional on this value, wages are also important in this function. This concept is similar to but distinct from the factor demand function, which is a function of prices and wages, not output.

a. Guaranteed investment contracts
b. Credible threat
c. Hicks-optimal outcome
d. Conditional factor demand

Chapter 5. Production

15. Economics:

- _____, the desire to own something and the ability to pay for it
- _____ curve, a graphic representation of a _____ schedule
- _____ deposit, the money in checking accounts
- _____ pull theory, the theory that inflation occurs when _____ for goods and services exceeds existing supplies
- _____ schedule, a table that lists the quantity of a good a person will buy it each different price
- _____ side economics, the school of economics at believes government spending and tax cuts open economy by raising _____

a. McKesson ' Robbins scandal
b. Demand
c. Variability
d. Production

16. In economics, an _____ is a contour line drawn through the set of points at which the same quantity of output is produced while changing the quantities of two or more inputs. While an indifference curve helps to answer the utility-maximizing problem of consumers, the _____ deals with the cost-minimization problem of producers. _____s are typically drawn on capital-labor graphs, showing the tradeoff between capital and labor in the production function, and the decreasing marginal returns of both inputs.

a. Economies of scale
b. Underinvestment employment relationship
c. Isoquant
d. Economic production quantity

17. In economics and finance, _____ is the change in total cost that arises when the quantity produced changes by one unit. It is the cost of producing one more unit of a good. Mathematically, the _____ function is expressed as the first derivative of the total cost (TC) function with respect to quantity (Q.)

a. Variable cost
b. Marginal cost
c. Quality costs
d. Khozraschyot

18. _____s are expenses that change in proportion to the activity of a business. In other words, _____ is the sum of marginal costs. It can also be considered normal costs.

a. Quality costs
b. Cost-Volume-Profit Analysis
c. Cost allocation
d. Variable cost

19. In economic models, the _____ time frame assumes no fixed factors of production. Firms can enter or leave the marketplace, and the cost (and availability) of land, labor, raw materials, and capital goods can be assumed to vary. In contrast, in the short-run time frame, certain factors are assumed to be fixed, because there is not sufficient time for them to change.

a. Productivity world
b. Price/performance ratio
c. Diseconomies of scale
d. Long-run

20. In economics, the concept of the _____ refers to the decision-making time frame of a firm in which at least one factor of production is fixed. Costs which are fixed in the _____ have no impact on a firms decisions. For example a firm can raise output by increasing the amount of labour through overtime.

Chapter 5. Production

a. Short-run
b. Product Pipeline
c. Hicks-neutral technical change
d. Productivity model

21. In economics, _____ is the total supply of goods and services produced by a national economy during a specific time period. It is the total amount of goods and services in the economy available at all possible price levels.
    a. Aggregation problem
    b. Aggregate demand
    c. Aggregate expenditure
    d. Aggregate supply

22. _____ is a branch of economics that uses microeconomic techniques to simultaneously determine allocative efficiency within an economy and the income distribution associated with it. It analyzes social welfare, however measured, in terms of economic activities of the individuals that comprise the theoretical society considered. As such, individuals, with associated economic activities, are the basic units for aggregating to social welfare, whether of a group, a community, or a society, and there is no 'social welfare' apart from the 'welfare' associated with its individual units.
    a. Tobit model
    b. Law of increasing costs
    c. Welfare economics
    d. General equilibrium

23. _____s is the social science that studies the production, distribution, and consumption of goods and services. The term _____s comes from the Ancient Greek οἰκονομία from οἶκος (oikos, 'house') + νόμος (nomos, 'custom' or 'law'), hence 'rules of the house(hold)'. Current _____ models developed out of the broader field of political economy in the late 19th century, owing to a desire to use an empirical approach more akin to the physical sciences.
    a. Opportunity cost
    b. Inflation
    c. Energy economics
    d. Economic

24. _____ has been defined as a process of dissecting an activity into its component parts and task sequence in order to identify its inherent properties and the skills required for its performance.
    a. Activity analysis
    b. AD-IA Model
    c. ACCRA Cost of Living Index
    d. ACEA agreement

25. In economics, an _____ uses a matrix representation of a nation's (or a region's) economy to predict the effect of changes in one industry on others and by consumers, government, and foreign suppliers on the economy. Wassily Leontief (1905-1999) is credited with the development of this analysis. Francois Quesnay developed a cruder version of this technique called Tableau économique.
    a. ACCRA Cost of Living Index
    b. ACEA agreement
    c. AD-IA Model
    d. Input-output model

Chapter 6. Choice Under Uncertainty

1. In economics, game theory, and decision theory the _____ theorem or _____ hypothesis predicts that the 'betting preferences' of people with regard to uncertain outcomes (gambles) can be described by a mathematical relation which takes into account the size of a payout (whether in money or other goods), the probability of occurrence, risk aversion, and the different utility of the same payout to people with different assets or personal preferences. It is a more sophisticated theory than simply predicting that choices will be made based on expected value (which takes into account only the size of the payout and the probability of occurrence.)

Daniel Bernoulli described the complete theory in 1738.

   a. Ordinal utility   b. Utility
   c. Expected utility hypothesis   d. Expected utility

2. _____ is a concept in economics, finance, and psychology related to the behaviour of consumers and investors under uncertainty. _____ is the reluctance of a person to accept a bargain with an uncertain payoff rather than another bargain with a more certain, but possibly lower, expected payoff. For example, a risk-averse investor might choose to put his or her money into a bank account with a low but guaranteed interest rate, rather than into a stock that is likely to have high returns, but also has a chance of becoming worthless.

   a. Risk aversion   b. Risk theory
   c. Compound annual growth rate   d. Reinsurance

3. _____ is a measure of the strength of a brand, product, service relative to competitive offerings. There is often a geographic element to the competitive landscape. In defining _____, you must see to what extent a product, brand, or firm controls a product category in a given geographic area.

   a. Horizontal territorial allocation   b. Demand shaping
   c. Price elasticity of supply   d. Market dominance

4. _____ means random.

A _____ process is one whose behavior is non-deterministic in that a system's subsequent state is determined both by the process's predictable actions and by a random element. _____ crafts are complex systems whose practitioners, even if complete experts, acknowledge that outcomes result from both known and unknown causes.

   a. 100-year flood   b. Theory
   c. 130-30 fund   d. Stochastic

5. In economics, _____ is a measure of the relative satisfaction from consumption of various goods and services. Given this measure, one may speak meaningfully of increasing or decreasing _____, and thereby explain economic behavior in terms of attempts to increase one's _____. For illustrative purposes, changes in _____ are sometimes expressed in units called utils.

   a. Utility function   b. Ordinal utility
   c. Expected utility hypothesis   d. Utility

Chapter 6. Choice Under Uncertainty

6. Economics:

   - _____,the desire to own something and the ability to pay for it
   - _____ curve,a graphic representation of a _____ schedule
   - _____ deposit, the money in checking accounts
   - _____ pull theory,the theory that inflation occurs when _____ for goods and services exceeds existing supplies
   - _____ schedule,a table that lists the quantity of a good a person will buy it each different price
   - _____ side economics,the school of economics at believes government spending and tax cuts open economy by raising _____

   a. Production
   b. Variability
   c. McKesson ' Robbins scandal
   d. Demand

7. _____ is a way of expressing knowledge or belief that an event will occur or has occurred. In mathematics the concept has been given an exact meaning in _____ theory, that is used extensively in such areas of study as mathematics, statistics, finance, gambling, science, and philosophy to draw conclusions about the likelihood of potential events and the underlying mechanics of complex systems.

The word _____ does not have a consistent direct definition.

   a. Probability
   b. 130-30 fund
   c. 1921 recession
   d. 100-year flood

8. While preferences are the conventional foundation of microeconomics, it is often convenient to represent preferences with a _____ and reason indirectly about preferences with _____s. Let X be the consumption set, the set of all mutually-exclusive packages the consumer could conceivably consume (such as an indifference curve map without the indifference curves.) The consumer's _____ $u : X \rightarrow \mathbf{R}$ ranks each package in the consumption set.
   a. Utility
   b. Ordinal utility
   c. Expected utility hypothesis
   d. Utility function

9. The _____ is a choice problem designed by Maurice Allais to show an inconsistency of actual observed choices with one assumption of expected utility theory. The assumption in question is the axiom of independence, which says that if people generally prefer lottery X over lottery Y, then mixing both lotteries with a third lottery, Z, should not alter the preference, i.e., if X > Y, then X + Z > Y + Z, where '>' indicates preference and '+' means offering the gambler the outcome of both lotteries.

The inconsistency Alias presented arises when comparing participants' choices in two different experiments he proposed, each of which consists of a choice between two gambles, A and B. The payoffs for each gamble in each experiment are as follows:

Average winnings of each gamble:

   Experiment 1:

Gamble 1A: $1,000,000 (Preferred) - The _____: Based on average winnings people should prefer 1B to 1A
Gamble 1B: $1,390,000 ($390,000 more than 1A)

Experiment 2:

    Gamble 2A: $110,000
    Gamble 2B: $500,000 ($390,000 more than 2A) (Preferred)

Allais asserted that, presented with the choice between 1A and 1B, most people would choose 1A, and presented with the choice between 2A and 2B, most people would choose 2B.

a. Allais paradox
b. Anecdotal value
c. ACCRA Cost of Living Index
d. ACEA agreement

10. The _____ is the apparent contradiction that although water is on the whole more useful, in terms of survival, than diamonds, diamonds command a higher price in the market. The economist Adam Smith is often considered to be the classic presenter of this paradox. Nicolaus Copernicus, John Locke, John Law and others had previously tried to explain the disparity.
a. St. Petersburg paradox
b. Paradox of value
c. 130-30 fund
d. 100-year flood

11. The term _____ is a neo-Latin word meaning 'before the event'. _____ is used most commonly in the commercial world, where results of a particular action, or series of actions, are forecast in advance. The opposite of _____ is ex-post.
a. ACCRA Cost of Living Index
b. ACEA agreement
c. AD-IA Model
d. Ex-ante

12. In probability theory and statistics, the _____ or just distribution function, completely describes the probability distribution of a real-valued random variable X. For every real number x, the _____ of X is given by

$$x \mapsto F_X(x) = P(X \leq x),$$

where the right-hand side represents the probability that the random variable X takes on a value less than or equal to x. The probability that X lies in the interval (a, b] is therefore $F_X(b) - F_X(a)$ if a < b.

If treating several random variables X, Y, ...

a. Cumulative distribution function
b. 1921 recession
c. 100-year flood
d. 130-30 fund

13. In molecular kinetic theory in physics, a particle's _____ is a function of seven variables, $f(x,y,z,t;v_x,v_y,v_z)$, which gives the number of particles per unit volume in phase space. It is the number of particles having approximately the velocity (v_x,v_y,v_z) near the place (x,y,z) and time (t). The usual normalization of the _____ is

$$n(x,y,z,t) = \int f\, dv_x\, dv_y\, dv_z$$

$$N(t) = \int n\, dx\, dy\, dz$$

Here, N is the total number of particles and n is the number density of particles - the number of particles per unit volume, or the density divided by the mass of individual particles.

a. Distribution function
b. 130-30 fund
c. 100-year flood
d. 1921 recession

14. In mathematics, an _____ is a statement about the relative size or order of two objects, or about whether they are the same or not

- The notation a < b means that a is less than b.
- The notation a > b means that a is greater than b.
- The notation a ≠ b means that a is not equal to b, but does not say that one is greater than the other or even that they can be compared in size.

In each statement above, a is not equal to b. These relations are known as strict inequalities. The notation a < b may also be read as 'a is strictly less than b'.

a. AD-IA Model
b. Inequality
c. ACCRA Cost of Living Index
d. ACEA agreement

15. _____, in law and economics, is a form of risk management primarily used to hedge against the risk of a contingent loss. _____ is defined as the equitable transfer of the risk of a loss, from one entity to another, in exchange for a premium, and can be thought of as a guaranteed small loss to prevent a large, possibly devastating loss. An insurer is a company selling the _____; an insured or policyholder is the person or entity buying the _____.

a. ACCRA Cost of Living Index
b. ACEA agreement
c. AD-IA Model
d. Insurance

16. In economics, an _____ uses a matrix representation of a nation's (or a region's) economy to predict the effect of changes in one industry on others and by consumers, government, and foreign suppliers on the economy. Wassily Leontief (1905-1999) is credited with the development of this analysis. Francois Quesnay developed a cruder version of this technique called Tableau économique.

a. AD-IA Model
b. Input-output model
c. ACCRA Cost of Living Index
d. ACEA agreement

17. In business and accounting, _____ are everything of value that is owned by a person or company. It is a claim on the property your income of a borrower. The balance sheet of a firm records the monetary value of the _____ owned by the firm.

   a. Amortization schedule
   b. ACEA agreement
   c. Assets
   d. ACCRA Cost of Living Index

18. _____ is the strategy an investor uses to distribute his or her investments among various classes of investment vehicles (e.g., stocks and bonds.)

A large part of financial planning is finding an _____ that is appropriate for a given person in terms of their appetite for and ability to shoulder risk. This can depend on various factors; see investor profile.

   a. Investor awareness
   b. Investing online
   c. Equity repositioning
   d. Asset allocation

19. In mathematics, a _____ is a constant multiplicative factor of a certain object. For example, in the expression $9x^2$, the _____ of x^2 is 9.

The object can be such things as a variable, a vector, a function, etc.

   a. 1921 recession
   b. Coefficient
   c. 130-30 fund
   d. 100-year flood

20. A _____ is a situation that involves losing one quality or aspect of something in return for gaining another quality or aspect. It implies a decision to be made with full comprehension of both the upside and downside of a particular choice.

In economics the term is expressed as opportunity cost, referring the most preferred alternative given up.

   a. Trade-off
   b. Whitemail
   c. Nonmarket
   d. Friedman-Savage utility function

21. _____ is a concept with somewhat disparate meanings in several fields. It also has a common meaning which has a loose connection with some of those more definite meanings.

Casually, it is typically used to denote a lack of order, or purpose, or cause.

   a. 100-year flood
   b. Randomness
   c. 1921 recession
   d. 130-30 fund

22. In mathematics, _____ are used in the study of chance and probability. They were developed to assist in the analysis of games of chance, stochastic events, and the results of scientific experiments by capturing only the mathematical properties necessary to answer probabilistic questions. Further formalizations have firmly grounded the entity in the theoretical domains of mathematics by making use of measure theory.

   a. 1921 recession
   b. 100-year flood
   c. 130-30 fund
   d. Random variables

Chapter 6. Choice Under Uncertainty

23. The _____ is a paradox in decision theory and experimental economics in which people's choices violate the expected utility hypothesis. It is generally taken to be evidence for ambiguity aversion. The paradox was popularized by Daniel Ellsberg, although a version of it was noted considerably earlier by John Maynard Keynes (Keynes 1921, pp.75-76, p.315, ft.2.)
   a. ACCRA Cost of Living Index
   b. Ellsberg paradox
   c. ACEA agreement
   d. AD-IA Model

24. _____ is a branch of applied mathematics that is used in the social sciences (most notably economics), biology, engineering, political science, international relations, computer science, and philosophy. _____ attempts to mathematically capture behavior in strategic situations, in which an individual's success in making choices depends on the choices of others. While initially developed to analyze competitions in which one individual does better at another's expense (zero sum games), it has been expanded to treat a wide class of interactions, which are classified according to several criteria.
   a. Discriminatory price auction
   b. Dollar auction
   c. Proper equilibrium
   d. Game theory

1. _____ is a branch of applied mathematics that is used in the social sciences (most notably economics), biology, engineering, political science, international relations, computer science, and philosophy. _____ attempts to mathematically capture behavior in strategic situations, in which an individual's success in making choices depends on the choices of others. While initially developed to analyze competitions in which one individual does better at another's expense (zero sum games), it has been expanded to treat a wide class of interactions, which are classified according to several criteria.
   a. Dollar auction
   b. Proper equilibrium
   c. Game theory
   d. Discriminatory price auction

Chapter 7. Basic Elements of Noncooperative Games 35

2. A _____ is:

- Rewrite _____, in generative grammar and computer science
- Standardization, a formal and widely-accepted statement, fact, definition, or qualification
- Operation, a determinate _____ for performing a mathematical operation and obtaining a certain result (Mathematics, Logic)
    - Unary operation
    - Binary operation
- _____ of inference, a function from sets of formulae to formulae (Mathematics, Logic)
- _____ of thumb, principle with broad application that is not intended to be strictly accurate or reliable for every situation. Also often simply referred to as a _____
- Moral, an atomic element of a moral code for guiding choices in human behavior
- Heuristic, a quantized '_____' which shows a tendency or probability for successful function
- A regulation, as in sports
- A Production _____, as in computer science
- Procedural law, a _____ set governing the application of laws to cases
    - A law, which may informally be called a '_____'
    - A court ruling, a decision by a court
- In the U.S. Government, a regulation mandated by Congress, but written or expanded upon by the Executive Branch.
- Norm (sociology), an informal but widely accepted _____, concept, truth, definition, or qualification (social norms, legal norms, coding norms)
- Norm (philosophy), a kind of sentence or a reason to act, feel or believe
- 'Rulership' is the concept of governance by a government:
    - Military _____, governance by a military body
    - Monastic _____, a collection of precepts that guides the life of monks or nuns in a religious order where the superior holds the place of Christ
- Slide _____

- '_____,' a song by Ayumi Hamasaki
- '_____,' a song by rapper Nas
- '_____s,' an album by the band The Whitest Boy Alive
- _____s: Pyaar Ka Superhit Formula, a 2003 Bollywood film
- ruler, an instrument for measuring lengths
- _____, a component of an astrolabe, circumferator or similar instrument
- The _____s, a bestselling self-help book
- _____ Project (Run Up-to-date Linux Everywhere), a project that aims to use up-to-date Linux software on old PCs
- _____ engine, a software system that helps managing business _____s
- Ja _____, a hip hop artist
    - R.U.L.E., a 2005 greatest hits album by rapper Ja _____
- '_____s,' a KMFDM song

a. Technocracy
c. Rule

b. Procter ' Gamble
d. Demand

3. _____ is the name for a simple example game used in game theory. It is the two strategy equivalent of Rock, Paper, Scissors. _____, also called the Pesky Little Brother Game or Parity Game, is used primarily to illustrate the concept of mixed strategies and a mixed strategy Nash equilibrium.
   a. Self-confirming equilibrium
   b. Contingent cooperator
   c. Potential game
   d. Matching Pennies

4. In combinatorial game theory, a _____ is a directed graph whose nodes are positions in a game and whose edges are moves. The complete _____ for a game is the _____ starting at the initial position and containing all possible moves from each position. The first two ply of the _____ for tic-tac-toe.

The diagram shows the first two levels, or ply, in the _____ for tic-tac-toe.

   a. Fuzzy game
   b. Game complexity
   c. Map-coloring games
   d. Game tree

5. The concept was first developed in game theory and consequently zero-sum situations are often called _____s though this does not imply that the concept applies only to what are commonly referred to as games.

For 2-player finite _____s, the different game theoretic Solution concepts of Nash equilibrium, minimax, and maximin all give the same solution. In the solution, players play a mixed strategy.

   a. Gordon growth model
   b. Cash or share options
   c. General purpose technologies
   d. Zero-sum Game

6. _____ is a term used in game theory. A game is said to have _____ if all players know all moves that have taken place.

Chess is an example of a game with _____ as each player can see all of the pieces on the board at all times.

   a. Game theory
   b. Perfect rationality
   c. Parity game
   d. Perfect information

7. In economics, _____ is a measure of the relative satisfaction from consumption of various goods and services. Given this measure, one may speak meaningfully of increasing or decreasing _____, and thereby explain economic behavior in terms of attempts to increase one's _____. For illustrative purposes, changes in _____ are sometimes expressed in units called utils.
   a. Expected utility hypothesis
   b. Ordinal utility
   c. Utility function
   d. Utility

8. While preferences are the conventional foundation of microeconomics, it is often convenient to represent preferences with a _____ and reason indirectly about preferences with _____s. Let X be the consumption set, the set of all mutually-exclusive packages the consumer could conceivably consume (such as an indifference curve map without the indifference curves.) The consumer's _____ $u : X \to \mathbf{R}$ ranks each package in the consumption set.
   a. Utility
   b. Utility function
   c. Expected utility hypothesis
   d. Ordinal utility

Chapter 7. Basic Elements of Noncooperative Games

9. In game theory, _____ is a way of describing a game. Unlike extensive form, normal-form representations are not graphical per se, but rather represent the game by way of a matrix. While this approach can be of greater use in identifying strictly dominated strategies and Nash equilibria, some information is lost as compared to extensive-form representations.

   a. Normal form
   b. 130-30 fund
   c. 100-year flood
   d. 1921 recession

10. _____ is an online peer-reviewed magazine published by the Agricultural ' Applied Economics Association (AAEA) for readers interested in the policy and management of agriculture, the food industry, natural resources, rural communities, and the environment. _____ is published quarterly and is available free online. It is currently one of three outreach products offered by AAEA, along with the more timely Policy Issues and the forthcoming Shared Materials section of the AAEA Web site.

   a. 100-year flood
   b. 1921 recession
   c. Choices
   d. 130-30 fund

11. In economics, game theory, and decision theory the _____ theorem or _____ hypothesis predicts that the 'betting preferences' of people with regard to uncertain outcomes (gambles) can be described by a mathematical relation which takes into account the size of a payout (whether in money or other goods), the probability of occurrence, risk aversion, and the different utility of the same payout to people with different assets or personal preferences. It is a more sophisticated theory than simply predicting that choices will be made based on expected value (which takes into account only the size of the payout and the probability of occurrence.)

Daniel Bernoulli described the complete theory in 1738.

   a. Expected utility
   b. Ordinal utility
   c. Expected utility hypothesis
   d. Utility

Chapter 8. Simultaneous-Move Games

1. In game theory, _____ is a solution concept of a game involving two or more players, in which each player is assumed to know the equilibrium strategies of the other players, and no player has anything to gain by changing only his or her own strategy unilaterally. If each player has chosen a strategy and no player can benefit by changing his or her strategy while the other players keep theirs unchanged, then the current set of strategy choices and the corresponding payoffs constitute a _____.

Stated simply, Amy and Bill are in _____ if Amy is making the best decision she can, taking into account Bill's decision, and Bill is making the best decision he can, taking into account Amy's decision.

a. Linear production game
b. Proper equilibrium
c. Lump of labour
d. Nash equilibrium

2. _____ is an economic model used to describe an industry structure in which companies compete on the amount of output they will produce, which they decide on independently of each other and at the same time. It is named after Antoine Augustin Cournot (1801-1877) after he observed competition in a spring water duopoly. It has the following features:

- There is more than one firm and all firms produce a homogeneous product, i.e. there is no product differentiation;
- Firms do not cooperate, i.e. there is no collusion;
- Firms have market power, i.e. each firm's output decision affects the good's price;
- The number of firms is fixed;
- Firms compete in quantities, and choose quantities simultaneously;
- The firms are economically rational and act strategically, usually seeking to maximize profit given their competitors' decisions.

An essential assumption of this model is that each firm aims to maximize profits, based on the expectation that its own output decision will not have an effect on the decisions of its rivals. Price is a commonly known decreasing function of total output.

a. Cournot competition
b. 130-30 fund
c. 1921 recession
d. 100-year flood

3. In economics, game theory, and decision theory the _____ theorem or _____ hypothesis predicts that the 'betting preferences' of people with regard to uncertain outcomes (gambles) can be described by a mathematical relation which takes into account the size of a payout (whether in money or other goods), the probability of occurrence, risk aversion, and the different utility of the same payout to people with different assets or personal preferences. It is a more sophisticated theory than simply predicting that choices will be made based on expected value (which takes into account only the size of the payout and the probability of occurrence.)

Daniel Bernoulli described the complete theory in 1738.

a. Expected utility hypothesis
b. Ordinal utility
c. Utility
d. Expected utility

4. In economics, _____ is a measure of the relative satisfaction from consumption of various goods and services. Given this measure, one may speak meaningfully of increasing or decreasing _____, and thereby explain economic behavior in terms of attempts to increase one's _____. For illustrative purposes, changes in _____ are sometimes expressed in units called utils.

a. Ordinal utility
b. Expected utility hypothesis
c. Utility function
d. Utility

5. While preferences are the conventional foundation of microeconomics, it is often convenient to represent preferences with a _____ and reason indirectly about preferences with _____s. Let X be the consumption set, the set of all mutually-exclusive packages the consumer could conceivably consume (such as an indifference curve map without the indifference curves.) The consumer's _____ $u : X \to \mathbf{R}$ ranks each package in the consumption set.
   a. Ordinal utility
   b. Utility function
   c. Utility
   d. Expected utility hypothesis

6. _____, or a _____ is the concept of a resulting effect (cf. cause and effect, arising from another action. In general terms, it is used to indicate that all human actions, particularly crime and sin, have profound effects.
   a. Solved
   b. Consequence
   c. Variability
   d. Rule

7. _____ is the name for a simple example game used in game theory. It is the two strategy equivalent of Rock, Paper, Scissors. _____, also called the Pesky Little Brother Game or Parity Game, is used primarily to illustrate the concept of mixed strategies and a mixed strategy Nash equilibrium.
   a. Contingent cooperator
   b. Potential game
   c. Self-confirming equilibrium
   d. Matching Pennies

8. In game theory, a _____ is a solution concept that is more general than the well known Nash equilibrium. It was first discussed by mathematician Robert Aumann (1974.) The idea is that each player chooses her action according to her observation of the value of the same public signal.
   a. Markov perfect
   b. Dollar auction
   c. Linear production game
   d. Correlated equilibrium

9. _____ is a term used in economics and game theory to describe an economic situation or game in which knowledge about other market participants or players is available to all participants. Every player knows the payoffs and strategies available to other players.

   _____ is one of the theoretical pre-conditions of an efficient perfectly competitive market.

   a. Metagame analysis
   b. Repeated game
   c. Replicator equation
   d. Complete information

10. In economics, the _____ is the change in consumption resulting from a change in real income.

Another important item that can change is the money income of the consumer. The _____ is the phenomenon observed through changes in purchasing power.

   a. Equilibrium wage
   b. Export subsidy
   c. Inflation hedge
   d. Income effect

Chapter 8. Simultaneous-Move Games

11. _____ refers to methods in probability and statistics named after the Reverend Thomas Bayes (ca. 1702-1761), in particular methods related to:

- the degree-of-belief interpretation of probability, as opposed to frequency or proportion or propensity interpretations; or
- Bayes' theorem on conditional probability.

These methods include:

- Bayes estimator
- Bayes factor
- _____ average
- _____ spam filtering
- _____ game
- _____ inference
- _____ information criterion
- _____ multivariate linear regression
    - _____ linear regression, a special case
- _____ model comparison
- _____ network
- _____ probability
- Empirical Bayes method
- Naive Bayes classifier

_____ also refers to the application of this probability theory to the functioning of the brain

- _____ brain

a. Fiscal
b. Technocracy
c. Freedom Park
d. Bayesian

12. In game theory, a _____ is one in which information about characteristics of the other players (i.e. payoffs) is incomplete. Following John C. Harsanyi's framework, a _____ can be modelled by introducing Nature as a player in a game. Nature assigns a random variable to each player which could take values of types for each player and associating probabilities or a probability density function with those types (in the course of the game, nature randomly chooses a type for each player according to the probability distribution across each player's type space.)

a. Sparse binary polynomial hashing
b. Strong prior
c. Random naive Bayes
d. Bayesian game

13. In game theory, the _____ was contributed by Nobel laureate John Harsanyi in 1973. The theorem aims to justify a puzzling aspect of mixed strategy Nash equilibria: that each player is wholly indifferent amongst each of the actions he puts non-zero weight on, yet he mixes them so as to make every other player also indifferent.

The mixed strategy equilibria are explained as being the limit of pure strategy equilibria for a disturbed game of incomplete information in which the payoffs of each player are known to themselves but not their opponents.

a. Bounded rationality
b. Solution concept
c. Drama theory
d. Purification theorem

14. In game theory, _____ is a way of describing a game. Unlike extensive form, normal-form representations are not graphical per se, but rather represent the game by way of a matrix. While this approach can be of greater use in identifying strictly dominated strategies and Nash equilibria, some information is lost as compared to extensive-form representations.
a. 1921 recession
b. Normal form
c. 100-year flood
d. 130-30 fund

15. A _____ is a type of sealed-bid auction, where bidders submit written bids without knowing the bid of the other people in the auction. The highest bidder wins, but the price paid is the second-highest bid. The auction was created by William Vickrey.
a. Box social
b. Vickrey auction
c. Mystery auction
d. Forward auction

16. _____ is a decision rule used in decision theory, game theory, statistics and philosophy for minimizing the maximum possible loss. Alternatively, it can be thought of as maximizing the minimum gain (maximin.) It started from two-player zero-sum game theory, covering both the cases where players take alternate moves and those where they make simultaneous moves.
a. Design Impact Measures
b. Minimax
c. 100-year flood
d. 130-30 fund

Chapter 9. Dynamic Games

1. _____ is the process of reasoning backwards in time, from the end of a problem or situation, to determine a sequence of optimal actions. It proceeds by first considering the last time a decision might be made and choosing what to do in any situation at that time. Using this information, one can then determine what to do at the second-to-last time of decision.
    a. 130-30 fund
    b. 100-year flood
    c. 1921 recession
    d. Backward induction

2. _____ is a term used in game theory. A game is said to have _____ if all players know all moves that have taken place.

Chess is an example of a game with _____ as each player can see all of the pieces on the board at all times.

   a. Perfect information
   b. Game theory
   c. Parity game
   d. Perfect rationality

3. In game theory, _____ is a solution concept of a game involving two or more players, in which each player is assumed to know the equilibrium strategies of the other players, and no player has anything to gain by changing only his or her own strategy unilaterally. If each player has chosen a strategy and no player can benefit by changing his or her strategy while the other players keep theirs unchanged, then the current set of strategy choices and the corresponding payoffs constitute a _____.

Stated simply, Amy and Bill are in _____ if Amy is making the best decision she can, taking into account Bill's decision, and Bill is making the best decision he can, taking into account Amy's decision.

   a. Lump of labour
   b. Nash equilibrium
   c. Linear production game
   d. Proper equilibrium

4. In game theory, a _____ is an extensive form game which consists in some number of repetitions of some base game (called a stage game.) The stage game is usually one of the well-studied 2-person games. It captures the idea that a player will have to take into account the impact of his current action on the future actions of other players; this is sometimes called his reputation.
   a. Repeated Game
   b. Pursuit-evasion
   c. Correlated equilibrium
   d. Quasi-perfect equilibrium

5. _____ refers to methods in probability and statistics named after the Reverend Thomas Bayes (ca. 1702-1761), in particular methods related to:

   - the degree-of-belief interpretation of probability, as opposed to frequency or proportion or propensity interpretations; or
   - Bayes' theorem on conditional probability.

These methods include:

- Bayes estimator
- Bayes factor
- _____ average
- _____ spam filtering
- _____ game
- _____ inference
- _____ information criterion
- _____ multivariate linear regression
  - _____ linear regression, a special case
- _____ model comparison
- _____ network
- _____ probability
- Empirical Bayes method
- Naive Bayes classifier

_____ also refers to the application of this probability theory to the functioning of the brain

- _____ brain

a. Freedom Park   b. Bayesian
c. Technocracy   d. Fiscal

6. _____ is a refinement of Nash Equilibrium for extensive form games due to David M. Kreps and Robert Wilson. A _____ specifies not only a strategy for each of the players but also a belief for each of the players. A belief gives, for each information set of the game belonging to the player, a probability distribution on the nodes in the information set.

a. Matching pennies   b. Pursuit-evasion
c. Markov strategy   d. Sequential equilibrium

7. _____ is a way of expressing knowledge or belief that an event will occur or has occurred. In mathematics the concept has been given an exact meaning in _____ theory, that is used extensively in such areas of study as mathematics, statistics, finance, gambling, science, and philosophy to draw conclusions about the likelihood of potential events and the underlying mechanics of complex systems.

The word _____ does not have a consistent direct definition.

a. 100-year flood   b. 130-30 fund
c. 1921 recession   d. Probability

8. In probability theory and statistics, a _____ identifies either the probability of each value of an unidentified random variable (when the variable is discrete), or the probability of the value falling within a particular interval (when the variable is continuous.) The _____ describes the range of possible values that a random variable can attain and the probability that the value of the random variable is within any (measurable) subset of that range. The Normal distribution, often called the 'bell curve'

When the random variable takes values in the set of real numbers, the _____ is completely described by the cumulative distribution function, whose value at each real x is the probability that the random variable is smaller than or equal to x.

a. 1921 recession
b. 130-30 fund
c. 100-year flood
d. Probability distribution

Chapter 9. Dynamic Games

9. A _____ is:

- Rewrite _____, in generative grammar and computer science
- Standardization, a formal and widely-accepted statement, fact, definition, or qualification
- Operation, a determinate _____ for performing a mathematical operation and obtaining a certain result (Mathematics, Logic)
    - Unary operation
    - Binary operation
- _____ of inference, a function from sets of formulae to formulae (Mathematics, Logic)
- _____ of thumb, principle with broad application that is not intended to be strictly accurate or reliable for every situation. Also often simply referred to as a _____
- Moral, an atomic element of a moral code for guiding choices in human behavior
- Heuristic, a quantized '_____' which shows a tendency or probability for successful function
- A regulation, as in sports
- A Production _____, as in computer science
- Procedural law, a _____ set governing the application of laws to cases
    - A law, which may informally be called a '_____'
    - A court ruling, a decision by a court
- In the U.S. Government, a regulation mandated by Congress, but written or expanded upon by the Executive Branch.
- Norm (sociology), an informal but widely accepted _____, concept, truth, definition, or qualification (social norms, legal norms, coding norms)
- Norm (philosophy), a kind of sentence or a reason to act, feel or believe
- 'Rulership' is the concept of governance by a government:
    - Military _____, governance by a military body
    - Monastic _____, a collection of precepts that guides the life of monks or nuns in a religious order where the superior holds the place of Christ
- Slide _____

- '_____,' a song by Ayumi Hamasaki
- '_____,' a song by rapper Nas
- '_____s,' an album by the band The Whitest Boy Alive
- _____s: Pyaar Ka Superhit Formula, a 2003 Bollywood film
- ruler, an instrument for measuring lengths
- _____, a component of an astrolabe, circumferator or similar instrument
- The _____s, a bestselling self-help book
- _____ Project (Run Up-to-date Linux Everywhere), a project that aims to use up-to-date Linux software on old PCs
- _____ engine, a software system that helps managing business _____s
- Ja _____, a hip hop artist
    - R.U.L.E., a 2005 greatest hits album by rapper Ja _____
- '_____s,' a KMFDM song

a. Technocracy
b. Rule
c. Procter ' Gamble
d. Demand

10. Competitive market equilibrium is the traditional concept of economic equilibrium, appropriate for the analysis of commodity markets with flexible prices and many traders, and serving as the benchmark of efficiency in economic analysis. It relies crucially on the assumption of a competitive environment where each trader decides upon a quantity that is so small compared to the total quantity traded in the market that their individual transactions have no influence on the prices. Competitive markets are an ideal, a standard that other market structures are evaluated by.

A _____ consists of a vector of prices and an allocation such that given the prices, each trader by maximizing his objective function (profit, preferences) subject to his technological possibilities and resource constraints plans to trade into his part of the proposed allocation, and such that the prices make all net trades compatible with one another ('clear the market') by equating aggregate supply and demand for the commodities which are traded.

- a. Partial equilibrium
- b. Product-Market Growth Matrix
- c. Market system
- d. Competitive equilibrium

11. _____ in economics and business is the result of an exchange and from that trade we assign a numerical monetary value to a good, service or asset. If Alice trades Bob 4 apples for an orange, the _____ of an orange is 4 apples. Inversely, the _____ of an apple is 1/4 oranges.
- a. Price war
- b. Price book
- c. Premium pricing
- d. Price

12. In game theory, _____ is a way of describing a game. Unlike extensive form, normal-form representations are not graphical per se, but rather represent the game by way of a matrix. While this approach can be of greater use in identifying strictly dominated strategies and Nash equilibria, some information is lost as compared to extensive-form representations.
- a. 1921 recession
- b. 100-year flood
- c. Normal form
- d. 130-30 fund

13. In economics, economic equilibrium is simply a state of the world where economic forces are balanced and in the absence of external influences the (equilibrium) values of economic variables will not change. It is the point at which quantity demanded and quantity supplied are equal. _____, for example, refers to a condition where a market price is established through competition such that the amount of goods or services sought by buyers is equal to the amount of goods or services produced by sellers.
- a. Product-Market Growth Matrix
- b. Regulated market
- c. Marketization
- d. Market equilibrium

14. In economics, a _____ exists when the production or use of goods and services by the market is not efficient. That is, there exists another outcome where all involved can be made better off. _____s can be viewed as scenarios where individuals' pursuit of pure self-interest leads to results that are not efficient - that can be improved upon from the societal point-of-view.
- a. Fixed exchange rate
- b. Market failure
- c. General equilibrium
- d. Financial economics

15. _____ is an important concept in economics with broad applications in game theory, engineering and the social sciences. The term is named after Vilfredo Pareto, an Italian economist who used the concept in his studies of economic efficiency and income distribution. Informally, pareto efficient situations are those in which any change to make any person better off would make someone else worse off.

Chapter 9. Dynamic Games

a. Pareto efficiency
b. Lump of labour
c. Perfect rationality
d. Matching pennies

16. Economics:

- _____, the desire to own something and the ability to pay for it
- _____ curve, a graphic representation of a _____ schedule
- _____ deposit, the money in checking accounts
- _____ pull theory, the theory that inflation occurs when _____ for goods and services exceeds existing supplies
- _____ schedule, a table that lists the quantity of a good a person will buy it each different price
- _____ side economics, the school of economics at believes government spending and tax cuts open economy by raising _____

a. Production
b. McKesson ' Robbins scandal
c. Demand
d. Variability

17. A _____ is a type of economic equilibrium, where the clearance on the market of some specific goods is obtained independently from prices and quantities demanded and supplied in other markets. In other words, the prices of all substitutes and complements, as well as income levels of consumers are constant. Here the dynamic process is that prices adjust until supply equals demand.
   a. Partial equilibrium
   b. Market depth
   c. Market system
   d. Horizontal market

18. _____s is the social science that studies the production, distribution, and consumption of goods and services. The term _____s comes from the Ancient Greek oá¼°κονομῖα from oá¼¶κος (oikos, 'house') + vÍŒμος (nomos, 'custom' or 'law'), hence 'rules of the house(hold)'. Current _____ models developed out of the broader field of political economy in the late 19th century, owing to a desire to use an empirical approach more akin to the physical sciences.
   a. Opportunity cost
   b. Economic
   c. Energy economics
   d. Inflation

19. _____ is a branch of economics that uses microeconomic techniques to simultaneously determine allocative efficiency within an economy and the income distribution associated with it. It analyzes social welfare, however measured, in terms of economic activities of the individuals that comprise the theoretical society considered. As such, individuals, with associated economic activities, are the basic units for aggregating to social welfare, whether of a group, a community, or a society, and there is no 'social welfare' apart from the 'welfare' associated with its individual units.
   a. General equilibrium
   b. Law of increasing costs
   c. Tobit model
   d. Welfare economics

Chapter 10. Competitive Markets

1. A _____ is something for which there is demand, but which is supplied without qualitative differentiation across a market. It is a product that is the same no matter who produces it, such as petroleum, notebook paper, or milk. In other words, copper is copper.
   a. 100-year flood
   b. Soft commodity
   c. Commodity
   d. Hard commodity

2. Competitive market equilibrium is the traditional concept of economic equilibrium, appropriate for the analysis of commodity markets with flexible prices and many traders, and serving as the benchmark of efficiency in economic analysis. It relies crucially on the assumption of a competitive environment where each trader decides upon a quantity that is so small compared to the total quantity traded in the market that their individual transactions have no influence on the prices.Competitive markets are an ideal, a standard that other market structures are evaluated by.

   A _____ consists of a vector of prices and an allocation such that given the prices, each trader by maximizing his objective function (profit, preferences) subject to his technological possibilities and resource constraints plans to trade into his part of the proposed allocation, and such that the prices make all net trades compatible with one another ('clear the market') by equating aggregate supply and demand for the commodities which are traded.

   a. Partial equilibrium
   b. Product-Market Growth Matrix
   c. Competitive equilibrium
   d. Market system

3. _____ is an important concept in economics with broad applications in game theory, engineering and the social sciences. The term is named after Vilfredo Pareto, an Italian economist who used the concept in his studies of economic efficiency and income distribution. Informally, pareto efficient situations are those in which any change to make any person better off would make someone else worse off.
   a. Perfect rationality
   b. Lump of labour
   c. Pareto efficiency
   d. Matching pennies

4. In economics, _____ refers to either

   1. a simplifying assumption made by the new classical school that markets always go to where the quantity supplied equals the quantity demanded; or
   2. the process of getting there via price adjustment.

   A _____ price is the price of a good or service at which quantity supplied is equal to quantity demanded. Also called the equilibrium price.

   In simple terms, this means that markets tend to move towards prices which balance the quantity supplied and the quantity demanded, such that the market will eventually be cleared of all surpluses and shortages (excess supply and demand.) The first version assumes that this process occurs instantaneously.

   a. Noise trader
   b. Market data
   c. Market portfolio
   d. Market clearing

5. _____ in economics and business is the result of an exchange and from that trade we assign a numerical monetary value to a good, service or asset. If Alice trades Bob 4 apples for an orange, the _____ of an orange is 4 apples. Inversely, the _____ of an apple is 1/4 oranges.

Chapter 10. Competitive Markets

a. Price book
b. Premium pricing
c. Price
d. Price war

6. In economics, _____ is the process by which a firm determines the price and output level that returns the greatest profit. There are several approaches to this problem. The total revenue--total cost method relies on the fact that profit equals revenue minus cost, and the marginal revenue--marginal cost method is based on the fact that total profit in a perfectly competitive market reaches its maximum point where marginal revenue equals marginal cost.
   a. Normal profit
   b. 100-year flood
   c. Profit margin
   d. Profit maximization

7. In economics, _____ is a measure of the relative satisfaction from consumption of various goods and services. Given this measure, one may speak meaningfully of increasing or decreasing _____, and thereby explain economic behavior in terms of attempts to increase one's _____. For illustrative purposes, changes in _____ are sometimes expressed in units called utils.
   a. Expected utility hypothesis
   b. Ordinal utility
   c. Utility function
   d. Utility

8. A _____ is a type of economic equilibrium, where the clearance on the market of some specific goods is obtained independently from prices and quantities demanded and supplied in other markets. In other words, the prices of all substitutes and complements, as well as income levels of consumers are constant. Here the dynamic process is that prices adjust until supply equals demand.
   a. Market system
   b. Partial equilibrium
   c. Market depth
   d. Horizontal market

9. In economics and finance, _____ is the change in total cost that arises when the quantity produced changes by one unit. It is the cost of producing one more unit of a good. Mathematically, the _____ function is expressed as the first derivative of the total cost (TC) function with respect to quantity (Q.)
   a. Khozraschyot
   b. Variable cost
   c. Marginal cost
   d. Quality costs

10. _____ is a common concept in economics, and gives rise to derived concepts such as consumer debt. Generally _____ is defined by opposition to production. But the precise definition can vary because different schools of economists define production quite differently.
    a. Federal Reserve Bank Notes
    b. Foreclosure data providers
    c. Cash or share options
    d. Consumption

11. In economics, _____ is the total demand for final goods and services in the economy (Y) at a given time and price level. It is the amount of goods and services in the economy that will be purchased at all possible price levels. This is the demand for the gross domestic product of a country when inventory levels are static.
    a. Aggregate expenditure
    b. Aggregate supply
    c. Aggregation problem
    d. Aggregate demand

12. In economics, _____ is the total supply of goods and services produced by a national economy during a specific time period. It is the total amount of goods and services in the economy available at all possible price levels.

Chapter 10. Competitive Markets

a. Aggregate expenditure
b. Aggregate demand
c. Aggregation problem
d. Aggregate supply

13. _____ is a broad label that refers to any individuals or households that use goods and services generated within the economy. The concept of a _____ is used in different contexts, so that the usage and significance of the term may vary.

Typically when business people and economists talk of _____s they are talking about person as _____, an aggregated commodity item with little individuality other than that expressed in the buy/not-buy decision.

a. 100-year flood
b. 1921 recession
c. Consumer
d. 130-30 fund

14. In economics and consumer theory, _____ functions are linear in one argument, generally the numeraire. Formally, for example, such a utility function could be written U(x,y) = u(x) + by, where b is a positive constant. Then if u'(x) > 0 and u''(x) < 0, the indifference curves are parallel.

a. Direct Market Access
b. Gross value added
c. False billing
d. Quasilinear utility

15. Economics:

- _____,the desire to own something and the ability to pay for it
- _____ curve,a graphic representation of a _____ schedule
- _____ deposit, the money in checking accounts
- _____ pull theory,the theory that inflation occurs when _____ for goods and services exceeds existing supplies
- _____ schedule,a table that lists the quantity of a good a person will buy it each different price
- _____ side economics,the school of economics at believes government spending and tax cuts open economy by raising _____

a. Production
b. Variability
c. McKesson ' Robbins scandal
d. Demand

16. While preferences are the conventional foundation of microeconomics, it is often convenient to represent preferences with a _____ and reason indirectly about preferences with _____s. Let X be the consumption set, the set of all mutually-exclusive packages the consumer could conceivably consume (such as an indifference curve map without the indifference curves.) The consumer's _____ $u : X \to \mathbf{R}$ ranks each package in the consumption set.

a. Utility
b. Expected utility hypothesis
c. Ordinal utility
d. Utility function

17. In economics, _____ is the comparison of two different equilibrium states, before and after a change in some underlying exogenous parameter. As a study of statics it compares two different unchanging points, after they have changed. It does not study the motion towards equilibrium, nor the process of the change itself.

a. Feasibility condition
b. Customer equity
c. Social surplus
d. Comparative statics

18. In economics, an _____ is a way of representing various distributions of resources. Edgeworth made his presentation in his famous book, Mathematical Psychics: An essay on the application of mathematics to the moral sciences, 1881. Edgeworth's original two axis depiction was developed into the now familiar box diagram by Pareto in 1906 and was popularized in a later exposition by Bowley.
a. Equivalent variation
b. Edgeworth box
c. ACCRA Cost of Living Index
d. International Social Security Association

19. A _____ is a consumption tax charged at the point of purchase for certain goods and services. The tax is usually set as a percentage by the government charging the tax. There is usually a list of exemptions.
a. 130-30 fund
b. Sales tax
c. 100-year flood
d. 1921 recession

20. To _____ is to impose a financial charge or other levy upon a taxpayer by a state or the functional equivalent of a state.

_____es are also imposed by many subnational entities. _____es consist of direct _____ or indirect _____, and may be paid in money or as its labour equivalent (often but not always unpaid.)

a. 1921 recession
b. 100-year flood
c. 130-30 fund
d. Tax

21. _____s is the social science that studies the production, distribution, and consumption of goods and services. The term _____s comes from the Ancient Greek oá¼°κονομῖα from oá¼¶κος (oikos, 'house') + νΌœμος (nomos, 'custom' or 'law'), hence 'rules of the house(hold)'. Current _____ models developed out of the broader field of political economy in the late 19th century, owing to a desire to use an empirical approach more akin to the physical sciences.
a. Opportunity cost
b. Inflation
c. Energy economics
d. Economic

22. In microeconomics, _____ is quite simply the conversion of inputs into outputs. It is an economic process that uses resources to create a good or service that is suitable for exchange. This can include manufacturing, storing, shipping, and packaging.
a. MET
b. Red Guards
c. Solved
d. Production

23. _____ is a branch of economics that uses microeconomic techniques to simultaneously determine allocative efficiency within an economy and the income distribution associated with it. It analyzes social welfare, however measured, in terms of economic activities of the individuals that comprise the theoretical society considered. As such, individuals, with associated economic activities, are the basic units for aggregating to social welfare, whether of a group, a community, or a society, and there is no 'social welfare' apart from the 'welfare' associated with its individual units.
a. General equilibrium
b. Welfare economics
c. Tobit model
d. Law of increasing costs

Chapter 10. Competitive Markets

24. _____ was a survey conducted by the U.S. Department of Justice to gauge the prevalence of alcohol and illegal drug use among prior arrestees. It was a reformulation of the prior Drug Use Forecasting (DUF) program, focused on five drugs in particular: cocaine, marijuana, methamphetamine, opiates, and PCP.

Participants were randomly selected from arrest records in major metropolitan areas; because no personally identifying information is taken from each record chosen, the resulting data can be correlated to arrest rates, but not to the total population of persons charged.

   a. AD-IA Model
   c. ACEA agreement
   b. Arrestee Drug Abuse Monitoring
   d. ACCRA Cost of Living Index

25. _____ was a Scottish moral philosopher and a pioneer of political economy. One of the key figures of the Scottish Enlightenment, Smith is the author of The Theory of Moral Sentiments and An Inquiry into the Nature and Causes of the Wealth of Nations. The latter, usually abbreviated as The Wealth of Nations, is considered his magnum opus and the first modern work of economics.
   a. Adolph Fischer
   c. Adam Smith
   b. Alan Greenspan
   d. Adolf Hitler

26. Loosely, the _____ is the change in the objective value of the optimal solution of an optimization problem obtained by relaxing the constraint by one unit. In a business application, a _____ is the maximum price that management is willing to pay for an extra unit of a given limited resource. For example, if a production line is already operating at its maximum 40 hour limit, the _____ would be the price of keeping the line operational for an additional hour.
   a. Shadow price
   c. 130-30 fund
   b. 100-year flood
   d. 1921 recession

27. A _____ provision refers to any program which seeks to provide a minimum level of income, service or other support for many marginalized groups such as the poor, elderly, and disabled people. _____ programs are undertaken by governments as well as non-governmental organizations (NGOs.) _____ payments and services are typically provided at the expense of taxpayers generally, funded by benefactors, or by compulsory enrollment of the poor themselves.
   a. 130-30 fund
   c. 1921 recession
   b. 100-year flood
   d. Social welfare

28. In economics, a _____ is a real-valued function that ranks conceivable social states (alternative complete descriptions of the society) from lowest to highest. Inputs of the function include any variables considered to affect welfare of the society (Sen, 1970, p. 33.)
   a. Gini coefficient
   c. Contract curve
   b. Frisch elasticity of labor supply
   d. Social welfare function

Chapter 10. Competitive Markets

29. _____ is an economic model used to describe an industry structure in which companies compete on the amount of output they will produce, which they decide on independently of each other and at the same time. It is named after Antoine Augustin Cournot (1801-1877) after he observed competition in a spring water duopoly. It has the following features:

- There is more than one firm and all firms produce a homogeneous product, i.e. there is no product differentiation;
- Firms do not cooperate, i.e. there is no collusion;
- Firms have market power, i.e. each firm's output decision affects the good's price;
- The number of firms is fixed;
- Firms compete in quantities, and choose quantities simultaneously;
- The firms are economically rational and act strategically, usually seeking to maximize profit given their competitors' decisions.

An essential assumption of this model is that each firm aims to maximize profits, based on the expectation that its own output decision will not have an effect on the decisions of its rivals. Price is a commonly known decreasing function of total output.

a. 1921 recession
b. 130-30 fund
c. 100-year flood
d. Cournot competition

30. In economics, a _____ is a graph of the costs of production as a function of total quantity produced. In a free market economy, productively efficient firms use these curves to find the optimal point of production, where they make the most profits. There are a few different types of _____s, each relevant to a different area of economics.

a. Kuznets curve
b. Cost curve
c. Demand curve
d. Phillips curve

31. In economics, a _____ is a loss of economic efficiency that can occur when equilibrium for a good or service is not Pareto optimal. In other words, either people who would have more marginal benefit than marginal cost are not buying the good or service, or people who would have more marginal cost than marginal benefit are buying the product.

Causes of _____ can include monopoly pricing, externalities, taxes or subsidies, and binding price ceilings or floors.

a. Deadweight loss
b. Leapfrogging
c. Distributive efficiency
d. Contract curve

32. There are two _____. The first states that any competitive equilibrium or Walrasian equilibrium leads to a Pareto efficient allocation of resources. The second states the converse, that any efficient allocation can be sustainable by a competitive equilibrium.

a. No-trade theorem
b. Stolper-Samuelson theorem
c. 100-year flood
d. Fundamental theorems of Welfare economics

33. The term surplus is used in economics for several related quantities. The _____ is the amount that consumers benefit by being able to purchase a product for a price that is less than they would be willing to pay. The producer surplus is the amount that producers benefit by selling at a market price mechanism that is higher than they would be willing to sell for.

a. Consumer surplus
b. Necessity good
c. Marginal rate of technical substitution
d. Microeconomic reform

34. The term surplus is used in economics for several related quantities. The consumer surplus is the amount that consumers benefit by being able to purchase a product for a price that is less than they would be willing to pay. The _____ is the amount that producers benefit by selling at a market price mechanism that is higher than they would be willing to sell for.
   a. Producer surplus
   b. Returns to scale
   c. Schedule delay
   d. Long term

35. _____ are the income that is gained by governments because of taxation of the people.

Just as there are different types of tax, the form in which _____ is collected also differs; furthermore, the agency that collects the tax may not be part of central government, but may be an alternative third-party licenced to collect tax which they themselves will use. For example:

- In the UK, the DVLA collects road tax, which is then passed on the treasury.

_____s on purchases can come from two forms: 'tax' itself is a percentage of the price added to the purchase (such as sales tax in US states, or VAT in the UK), while 'duty' is a fixed amount added to the purchase price (such as is commonly found on cigarettes.) In order to calculate the total tax raised from these sales, we must work out the effective tax rate multiplied by the quantity supplied.

   a. Taxable wage
   b. Tax and spend
   c. Taxation as slavery
   d. Tax revenue

36. In welfare economics, the _____ refers to a decision rule used to select between pairs of alternative feasible social states. One of these states is the hypothetical point of departure ('the original state'.) According to the _____, if the prospective gainers could compensate (any) prospective losers and leave no one worse off, the other state is to be selected (Chipman, 1987, p.
   a. Structural adjustment loan
   b. Missing market
   c. Triple bottom line
   d. Compensation principle

37. _____ is a term used by economists to describe a condition in which firms can freely enter the market for an economic good by establishing production and beginning to sell the product.

_____ is implied by the perfect competition condition that there is an unlimited number of buyers and sellers in a market. In comparison to perfect competition, however, _____ is a condition often more applicable to real world conditions.

   a. 100-year flood
   b. 1921 recession
   c. Free entry
   d. 130-30 fund

Chapter 10. Competitive Markets

38. In economic models, the _____ time frame assumes no fixed factors of production. Firms can enter or leave the marketplace, and the cost (and availability) of land, labor, raw materials, and capital goods can be assumed to vary. In contrast, in the short-run time frame, certain factors are assumed to be fixed, because there is not sufficient time for them to change.
   a. Diseconomies of scale
   b. Long-run
   c. Price/performance ratio
   d. Productivity world

39. In economics, the concept of the _____ refers to the decision-making time frame of a firm in which at least one factor of production is fixed. Costs which are fixed in the _____ have no impact on a firms decisions. For example a firm can raise output by increasing the amount of labour through overtime.
   a. Hicks-neutral technical change
   b. Short-run
   c. Product Pipeline
   d. Productivity model

40. In microeconomics, a consumer's _____ is the demand of a consumer over a bundle of goods that minimizes their expenditure while delivering a fixed level of utility. The function is named after John Hicks.

Mathematically,

$$h(p, \bar{u}) = \arg\min_x \sum_i p_i x_i$$
$$\text{such that} \quad u(x) > \bar{u}$$

where h is the _____, or commodity bundle demanded, at price level p and utility level $\bar{u}$.

   a. Hicksian demand function
   b. Kinked demand
   c. Kinked demand curve
   d. Precautionary demand

41. The _____ is an economic term, referring to an increase in spending that accompanies an increase or perceived increase in wealth.

The effect would cause changes in the amounts and composition of consumer consumption caused by changes in consumer wealth. People should spend more when one of two things is true: when people actually are richer (by objective measurement, for example, a bonus or a pay raise at work, which would be an income effect), or when people perceive themselves to be 'richer' (for example, the assessed value of their home increases, or a stock they own has gone up in price recently.)

   a. 130-30 fund
   b. Wealth effect
   c. 100-year flood
   d. Wealth condensation

42. In economics, the _____ can be defined as the graph depicting the relationship between the price of a certain commodity, and the amount of it that consumers are willing and able to purchase at that given price. It is a graphic representation of a demand schedule. The _____ for all consumers together follows from the _____ of every individual consumer: the individual demands at each price are added together.

a. Kuznets curve b. Wage curve
c. Cost curve d. Demand curve

Chapter 11. Externalities and Public Goods

1. In economics, an _____ or spillover of an economic transaction is an impact on a party that is not directly involved in the transaction. In such a case, prices do not reflect the full costs or benefits in production or consumption of a product or service. A positive impact is called an external benefit, while a negative impact is called an external cost.
   a. Environmental tariff
   b. Existence value
   c. Environmental impact assessment
   d. Externality

2. In economics, a _____ exists when the production or use of goods and services by the market is not efficient. That is, there exists another outcome where all involved can be made better off. _____s can be viewed as scenarios where individuals' pursuit of pure self-interest leads to results that are not efficient - that can be improved upon from the societal point-of-view.
   a. General equilibrium
   b. Market failure
   c. Financial economics
   d. Fixed exchange rate

3. _____ is an important concept in economics with broad applications in game theory, engineering and the social sciences. The term is named after Vilfredo Pareto, an Italian economist who used the concept in his studies of economic efficiency and income distribution. Informally, pareto efficient situations are those in which any change to make any person better off would make someone else worse off.
   a. Pareto efficiency
   b. Lump of labour
   c. Perfect rationality
   d. Matching pennies

4. In economics, a _____ is a good that is non-rivaled and non-excludable. This means, respectively, that consumption of the good by one individual does not reduce availability of the good for consumption by others; and that no one can be effectively excluded from using the good. In the real world, there may be no such thing as an absolutely non-rivaled and non-excludable good; but economists think that some goods approximate the concept closely enough for the analysis to be economically useful.
   a. Happiness economics
   b. Public good
   c. Neoclassical synthesis
   d. Demand-pull theory

5. _____s is the social science that studies the production, distribution, and consumption of goods and services. The term _____s comes from the Ancient Greek οἰκονομία from οἶκος (oikos, 'house') + νόμος (nomos, 'custom' or 'law'), hence 'rules of the house(hold)'. Current _____ models developed out of the broader field of political economy in the late 19th century, owing to a desire to use an empirical approach more akin to the physical sciences.
   a. Energy economics
   b. Inflation
   c. Opportunity cost
   d. Economic

6. A _____ is an object whose consumption increases the utility of the consumer, for which the quantity demanded exceeds the quantity supplied at zero price. _____s are usually modeled as having diminishing marginal utility. The first individual purchase has high utility; the second has less.
   a. Pie method
   b. Composite good
   c. Merit good
   d. Good

7. _____ is a branch of economics that uses microeconomic techniques to simultaneously determine allocative efficiency within an economy and the income distribution associated with it. It analyzes social welfare, however measured, in terms of economic activities of the individuals that comprise the theoretical society considered. As such, individuals, with associated economic activities, are the basic units for aggregating to social welfare, whether of a group, a community, or a society, and there is no 'social welfare' apart from the 'welfare' associated with its individual units.

a. Law of increasing costs
b. Welfare economics
c. General equilibrium
d. Tobit model

8. A _____ is an externality which operates through prices rather than through real resource effects. For example, an influx of city-dwellers buying second homes in a rural area can drive up house prices, making it difficult for young people in the area to get onto the property ladder.

This is in contrast with technical or real externalities which have a direct resource effect on a third party.

a. Guaranteed Maximum Price
b. Discounts and allowances
c. Pecuniary externality
d. Pricing

9. In economics, _____ is a measure of the relative satisfaction from consumption of various goods and services. Given this measure, one may speak meaningfully of increasing or decreasing _____, and thereby explain economic behavior in terms of attempts to increase one's _____. For illustrative purposes, changes in _____ are sometimes expressed in units called utils.

a. Expected utility hypothesis
b. Ordinal utility
c. Utility function
d. Utility

10. While preferences are the conventional foundation of microeconomics, it is often convenient to represent preferences with a _____ and reason indirectly about preferences with _____s. Let X be the consumption set, the set of all mutually-exclusive packages the consumer could conceivably consume (such as an indifference curve map without the indifference curves.) The consumer's _____ $u : X \rightarrow \mathbf{R}$ ranks each package in the consumption set.

a. Ordinal utility
b. Expected utility hypothesis
c. Utility
d. Utility function

11. Economics:

- _____, the desire to own something and the ability to pay for it
- _____ curve, a graphic representation of a _____ schedule
- _____ deposit, the money in checking accounts
- _____ pull theory, the theory that inflation occurs when _____ for goods and services exceeds existing supplies
- _____ schedule, a table that lists the quantity of a good a person will buy it each different price
- _____ side economics, the school of economics at believes government spending and tax cuts open economy by raising _____

a. Variability
b. Demand
c. McKesson ' Robbins scandal
d. Production

12. In economics and consumer theory, _____ functions are linear in one argument, generally the numeraire. Formally, for example, such a utility function could be written U(x,y) = u(x) + by, where b is a positive constant. Then if u'(x) > 0 and u''(x) < 0, the indifference curves are parallel.

Chapter 11. Externalities and Public Goods

a. False billing
c. Direct Market Access
b. Quasilinear utility
d. Gross value added

13. To _____ is to impose a financial charge or other levy upon a taxpayer by a state or the functional equivalent of a state.

_____es are also imposed by many subnational entities. _____es consist of direct _____ or indirect _____, and may be paid in money or as its labour equivalent (often but not always unpaid.)

a. 1921 recession
c. 100-year flood
b. 130-30 fund
d. Tax

14. To tax is to impose a financial charge or other levy upon a taxpayer by a state or the functional equivalent of a state.

_____ are also imposed by many subnational entities. _____ consist of direct tax or indirect tax, and may be paid in money or as its labour equivalent (often but not always unpaid.)

a. 1921 recession
c. 100-year flood
b. 130-30 fund
d. Taxes

15. A _____ is the exclusive authority to determine how a resource is used, whether that resource is owned by government or by individuals. All economic goods have a _____s attribute. This attribute has three broad components

1. The right to use the good
2. The right to earn income from the good
3. The right to transfer the good to others

The concept of _____s as used by economists and legal scholars are related but distinct. The distinction is largely seen in the economists' focus on the ability of an individual or collective to control the use of the good.

a. Property right
c. High-reeve
b. Holder in due course
d. Post-sale restraint

16. In law and economics, the _____, describes the economic efficiency of an economic allocation or outcome in the presence of externalities. The theorem states that when trade in an externality is possible and there are no transaction costs, bargaining will lead to an efficient outcome regardless of the initial allocation of property rights. In practice, obstacles to bargaining or poorly defined property rights can prevent Coasian bargaining.

a. Coase theorem
c. General Mining Act of 1872
b. Prior appropriation water rights
d. Means test

17. A _____ is a type of economic equilibrium, where the clearance on the market of some specific goods is obtained independently from prices and quantities demanded and supplied in other markets. In other words, the prices of all substitutes and complements, as well as income levels of consumers are constant. Here the dynamic process is that prices adjust until supply equals demand.

Chapter 11. Externalities and Public Goods

a. Market system
b. Horizontal market
c. Market depth
d. Partial equilibrium

18. A _____ is a situation in microeconomics where a competitive market allowing the exchange of a commodity would be Pareto-efficient, but no such market exists.

A variety of factors can lead to _____s:

A classic example of a _____ is the case of an externality like pollution, where decision makers are not responsible for some of the consequences of their actions. When a factory discharges polluted water into a river, that pollution can hurt people who fish in or get their drinking water from the river downstream, but the factory owner may have no incentive to consider those consequences.

a. Deadweight loss
b. Wage share
c. Distributive efficiency
d. Missing market

19. Competitive market equilibrium is the traditional concept of economic equilibrium, appropriate for the analysis of commodity markets with flexible prices and many traders, and serving as the benchmark of efficiency in economic analysis. It relies crucially on the assumption of a competitive environment where each trader decides upon a quantity that is so small compared to the total quantity traded in the market that their individual transactions have no influence on the prices. Competitive markets are an ideal, a standard that other market structures are evaluated by.

A _____ consists of a vector of prices and an allocation such that given the prices, each trader by maximizing his objective function (profit, preferences) subject to his technological possibilities and resource constraints plans to trade into his part of the proposed allocation, and such that the prices make all net trades compatible with one another ('clear the market') by equating aggregate supply and demand for the commodities which are traded.

a. Partial equilibrium
b. Product-Market Growth Matrix
c. Market system
d. Competitive equilibrium

20. _____ in economics and business is the result of an exchange and from that trade we assign a numerical monetary value to a good, service or asset. If Alice trades Bob 4 apples for an orange, the _____ of an orange is 4 apples. Inversely, the _____ of an apple is 1/4 oranges.

a. Premium pricing
b. Price war
c. Price
d. Price book

21. In game theory, _____ is a solution concept of a game involving two or more players, in which each player is assumed to know the equilibrium strategies of the other players, and no player has anything to gain by changing only his or her own strategy unilaterally. If each player has chosen a strategy and no player can benefit by changing his or her strategy while the other players keep theirs unchanged, then the current set of strategy choices and the corresponding payoffs constitute a _____.

Stated simply, Amy and Bill are in _____ if Amy is making the best decision she can, taking into account Bill's decision, and Bill is making the best decision he can, taking into account Amy's decision.

a. Lump of labour
c. Linear production game
b. Proper equilibrium
d. Nash equilibrium

22. _____ is a common concept in economics, and gives rise to derived concepts such as consumer debt. Generally _____ is defined by opposition to production. But the precise definition can vary because different schools of economists define production quite differently.
   a. Cash or share options
   c. Foreclosure data providers
   b. Federal Reserve Bank Notes
   d. Consumption

23. The _____ is an important result in mechanism design and the economics of asymmetric information. Informally, the result says that there is no efficient way for two parties to trade a good when they each have secret and probabilistically varying valuations for it, without the risk of forcing one party to trade at a loss.

Formally, the theorem applies if a prospective buyer A has a valuation $v_A \in [x_a, y_a]$, and the prospective seller B has an independent valuation $v_B \in [x_b, y_b]$, such that the intervals [x_a,y_a] and [x_b,y_b] overlap, and the probability densities for the valuations are strictly positive on those intervals.

   a. 100-year flood
   c. Myerson-Satterthwaite theorem
   b. 1921 recession
   d. 130-30 fund

24. In economics and finance, _____ is the change in total cost that arises when the quantity produced changes by one unit. It is the cost of producing one more unit of a good. Mathematically, the _____ function is expressed as the first derivative of the total cost (TC) function with respect to quantity (Q.)
   a. Variable cost
   c. Marginal cost
   b. Quality costs
   d. Khozraschyot

25. In calculus, a function f defined on a subset of the real numbers with real values is called _____, if for all x and y such that x >≤ y one has f(x) >≤ f(y), so f preserves the order. In layman's terms, the sign of the slope is always positive (the curve tending upwards) or zero (i.e., non-decreasing, or asymptotic, or depicted as a horizontal, flat line) Likewise, a function is called monotonically decreasing (non-increasing) if, whenever x >≤ y, then f(x) >≥ f(y), so it reverses the order.
   a. 130-30 fund
   c. 100-year flood
   b. 1921 recession
   d. Monotonic

Chapter 12. Market Power

1. In economics, _____ is the ability of a firm to alter the market price of a good or service. A firm with _____ can raise prices without losing all customers to competitors.

   When a firm has _____ it faces a downward-sloping demand curve.

   a. Price makers
   b. Market power
   c. Revenue-cap regulation
   d. Pacman conjecture

2. An _____ is a market form in which a market or industry is dominated by a small number of sellers (oligopolists.) Because there are few participants in this type of market, each oligopolist is aware of the actions of the others. The decisions of one firm influence, and are influenced by, the decisions of other firms.
   a. ACCRA Cost of Living Index
   b. ACEA agreement
   c. Oligopsony
   d. Oligopoly

3. In economics, a _____ exists when a specific individual or enterprise has sufficient control over a particular product or service to determine significantly the terms on which other individuals shall have access to it. Monopolies are thus characterized by a lack of economic competition for the good or service that they provide and a lack of viable substitute goods. The verb 'monopolize' refers to the process by which a firm gains persistently greater market share than what is expected under perfect competition.
   a. Monopoly
   b. 100-year flood
   c. 130-30 fund
   d. 1921 recession

4. _____ is one of the four Ps of the marketing mix. The other three aspects are product, promotion, and place. It is also a key variable in microeconomic price allocation theory.
   a. Point of total assumption
   b. Premium pricing
   c. Guaranteed Maximum Price
   d. Pricing

5. In economics, a _____ is a loss of economic efficiency that can occur when equilibrium for a good or service is not Pareto optimal. In other words, either people who would have more marginal benefit than marginal cost are not buying the good or service, or people who would have more marginal cost than marginal benefit are buying the product.

   Causes of _____ can include monopoly pricing, externalities, taxes or subsidies, and binding price ceilings or floors.

   a. Deadweight loss
   b. Leapfrogging
   c. Distributive efficiency
   d. Contract curve

6. In economics and finance, _____ is the change in total cost that arises when the quantity produced changes by one unit. It is the cost of producing one more unit of a good. Mathematically, the _____ function is expressed as the first derivative of the total cost (TC) function with respect to quantity (Q.)
   a. Variable cost
   b. Quality costs
   c. Khozraschyot
   d. Marginal cost

7. In microeconomics, _____ is the extra revenue that an additional unit of product will bring. It is the additional income from selling one more unit of a good; sometimes equal to price. It can also be described as the change in total revenue/change in number of units sold.

a. Long term
b. Market demand schedule
c. Reservation price
d. Marginal revenue

8. A _____ is something for which there is demand, but which is supplied without qualitative differentiation across a market. It is a product that is the same no matter who produces it, such as petroleum, notebook paper, or milk. In other words, copper is copper.

a. 100-year flood
b. Soft commodity
c. Hard commodity
d. Commodity

9. Economics:

- _____,the desire to own something and the ability to pay for it
- _____ curve,a graphic representation of a _____ schedule
- _____ deposit, the money in checking accounts
- _____ pull theory,the theory that inflation occurs when _____ for goods and services exceeds existing supplies
- _____ schedule,a table that lists the quantity of a good a person will buy it each different price
- _____ side economics,the school of economics at believes government spending and tax cuts open economy by raising _____

a. Demand
b. Production
c. Variability
d. McKesson ' Robbins scandal

10. _____ is an economic model used to describe an industry structure in which companies compete on the amount of output they will produce, which they decide on independently of each other and at the same time. It is named after Antoine Augustin Cournot (1801-1877) after he observed competition in a spring water duopoly. It has the following features:

- There is more than one firm and all firms produce a homogeneous product, i.e. there is no product differentiation;
- Firms do not cooperate, i.e. there is no collusion;
- Firms have market power, i.e. each firm's output decision affects the good's price;
- The number of firms is fixed;
- Firms compete in quantities, and choose quantities simultaneously;
- The firms are economically rational and act strategically, usually seeking to maximize profit given their competitors' decisions.

An essential assumption of this model is that each firm aims to maximize profits, based on the expectation that its own output decision will not have an effect on the decisions of its rivals. Price is a commonly known decreasing function of total output.

a. 130-30 fund
b. 1921 recession
c. 100-year flood
d. Cournot competition

11. In economics and consumer theory, _____ functions are linear in one argument, generally the numeraire. Formally, for example, such a utility function could be written U(x,y) = u(x) + by, where b is a positive constant. Then if $u'(x) > 0$ and $u''(x) < 0$, the indifference curves are parallel.

Chapter 12. Market Power

a. Gross value added
b. False billing
c. Quasilinear utility
d. Direct Market Access

12. In economics, _____ is a measure of the relative satisfaction from consumption of various goods and services. Given this measure, one may speak meaningfully of increasing or decreasing _____, and thereby explain economic behavior in terms of attempts to increase one's _____. For illustrative purposes, changes in _____ are sometimes expressed in units called utils.

a. Utility
b. Ordinal utility
c. Utility function
d. Expected utility hypothesis

13. While preferences are the conventional foundation of microeconomics, it is often convenient to represent preferences with a _____ and reason indirectly about preferences with _____s. Let X be the consumption set, the set of all mutually-exclusive packages the consumer could conceivably consume (such as an indifference curve map without the indifference curves.) The consumer's _____ $u : X \to \mathbf{R}$ ranks each package in the consumption set.

a. Ordinal utility
b. Utility
c. Expected utility hypothesis
d. Utility function

14. In game theory, _____ is a solution concept of a game involving two or more players, in which each player is assumed to know the equilibrium strategies of the other players, and no player has anything to gain by changing only his or her own strategy unilaterally. If each player has chosen a strategy and no player can benefit by changing his or her strategy while the other players keep theirs unchanged, then the current set of strategy choices and the corresponding payoffs constitute a _____.

Stated simply, Amy and Bill are in _____ if Amy is making the best decision she can, taking into account Bill's decision, and Bill is making the best decision he can, taking into account Amy's decision.

a. Proper equilibrium
b. Lump of labour
c. Linear production game
d. Nash equilibrium

15. _____ in economics and business is the result of an exchange and from that trade we assign a numerical monetary value to a good, service or asset. If Alice trades Bob 4 apples for an orange, the _____ of an orange is 4 apples. Inversely, the _____ of an apple is 1/4 oranges.

a. Price
b. Price book
c. Premium pricing
d. Price war

16. In marketing, _____ is the process of distinguishing the differences of a product or offering from others, to make it more attractive to a particular target market. This involves differentiating it from competitors' products as well as one's own product offerings.

Differentiation is a source of competitive advantage.

a. Market segment
b. Pricing science
c. Technology acceptance model
d. Product differentiation

17. In economics, _____ and economies of scale are related terms that describe what happens as the scale of production increases. They are different terms and should not be used interchangeably.

Chapter 12. Market Power

_____ refers to a technical property of production that examines changes in output subsequent to a proportional change in all inputs (where all inputs increase by a constant factor.)

a. Customer equity
c. Returns to scale

b. Necessity good
d. Constant returns to scale

18. In production, returns to scale refers to changes in output subsequent to a proportional change in all inputs (where all inputs increase by a constant factor.) If output increases by that same proportional change then there are _____ If output increases by less than that proportional change, there are decreasing returns to scale (DRS.)

a. Consumer sovereignty
c. Long term

b. Lexicographic preferences
d. Constant returns to scale

19. _____ is the controlled distribution of resources and scarce goods or services. _____ controls the size of the ration, one's allotted portion of the resources being distributed on a particular day or at a particular time.

In economics, it is often common to use the word '_____' to refer to one of the roles that prices play in markets, while _____ is called 'non-price _____.' Using prices to ration means that those with the most money (or other assets) and who want a product the most are first to receive it.

a. Rationing
c. 1921 recession

b. 100-year flood
d. 130-30 fund

20. A true _____ is a specific type of oligopoly where only two producers exist in one market. In reality, this definition is generally used where only two firms have dominant control over a market. In the field of industrial organization, it is the most commonly studied form of oligopoly due to its simplicity.

a. 130-30 fund
c. Duopoly

b. Megacorpstate
d. 100-year flood

Chapter 12. Market Power

21. A _____ is:

- Rewrite _____, in generative grammar and computer science
- Standardization, a formal and widely-accepted statement, fact, definition, or qualification
- Operation, a determinate _____ for performing a mathematical operation and obtaining a certain result (Mathematics, Logic)
    - Unary operation
    - Binary operation
- _____ of inference, a function from sets of formulae to formulae (Mathematics, Logic)
- _____ of thumb, principle with broad application that is not intended to be strictly accurate or reliable for every situation. Also often simply referred to as a _____
- Moral, an atomic element of a moral code for guiding choices in human behavior
- Heuristic, a quantized '_____' which shows a tendency or probability for successful function
- A regulation, as in sports
- A Production _____, as in computer science
- Procedural law, a _____ set governing the application of laws to cases
    - A law, which may informally be called a '_____'
    - A court ruling, a decision by a court
- In the U.S. Government, a regulation mandated by Congress, but written or expanded upon by the Executive Branch.
- Norm (sociology), an informal but widely accepted _____, concept, truth, definition, or qualification (social norms, legal norms, coding norms)
- Norm (philosophy), a kind of sentence or a reason to act, feel or believe
- 'Rulership' is the concept of governance by a government:
    - Military _____, governance by a military body
    - Monastic _____, a collection of precepts that guides the life of monks or nuns in a religious order where the superior holds the place of Christ
- Slide _____

- '_____,' a song by Ayumi Hamasaki
- '_____,' a song by rapper Nas
- '_____s,' an album by the band The Whitest Boy Alive
- _____s: Pyaar Ka Superhit Formula, a 2003 Bollywood film
- ruler, an instrument for measuring lengths
- _____, a component of an astrolabe, circumferator or similar instrument
- The _____s, a bestselling self-help book
- _____ Project (Run Up-to-date Linux Everywhere), a project that aims to use up-to-date Linux software on old PCs
- _____ engine, a software system that helps managing business _____s
- Ja _____, a hip hop artist
    - R.U.L.E., a 2005 greatest hits album by rapper Ja _____
- '_____s,' a KMFDM song

a. Procter ' Gamble
b. Rule
c. Technocracy
d. Demand

Chapter 12. Market Power

22. In economics, _____ is the total demand for final goods and services in the economy (Y) at a given time and price level. It is the amount of goods and services in the economy that will be purchased at all possible price levels. This is the demand for the gross domestic product of a country when inventory levels are static.
    a. Aggregate expenditure
    b. Aggregate supply
    c. Aggregation problem
    d. Aggregate demand

23. _____ is a broad label that refers to any individuals or households that use goods and services generated within the economy. The concept of a _____ is used in different contexts, so that the usage and significance of the term may vary.

    Typically when business people and economists talk of _____s they are talking about person as _____, an aggregated commodity item with little individuality other than that expressed in the buy/not-buy decision.

    a. 130-30 fund
    b. 100-year flood
    c. 1921 recession
    d. Consumer

24. _____ is a common market structure where many competing producers sell products that are differentiated from one another (ie. the products are substitutes, but are not exactly alike.) Many markets are monopolistically competitive, common examples include the markets for restaurants, cereal, clothing, shoes and service industries in large cities.
    a. Financial crisis
    b. Perfect competition
    c. Monopolistic competition
    d. Mathematical economics

25. In game theory, a _____ is an extensive form game which consists in some number of repetitions of some base game (called a stage game.) The stage game is usually one of the well-studied 2-person games. It captures the idea that a player will have to take into account the impact of his current action on the future actions of other players; this is sometimes called his reputation.
    a. Correlated equilibrium
    b. Quasi-perfect equilibrium
    c. Pursuit-evasion
    d. Repeated game

26. _____ refers to the state of not requiring any outside aid, support for survival; it is therefore a type of personal or collective autonomy. On a large scale, a totally self-sufficient economy that does not trade with the outside world is called an autarky.

    The term _____ is usually applied to varieties of sustainable living in which nothing is consumed outside of what is produced by the self-sufficient individuals.

    a. Sustainable forest management
    b. Self-sufficiency
    c. Sustainability science
    d. Global Reporting Initiative

27. Discounting is a financial mechanism in which a debtor obtains the right to delay payments to a creditor, for a defined period of time, in exchange for a charge or fee. Essentially, the party that owes money in the present purchases the right to delay the payment until some future date. The _____, or charge, is simply the difference between the original amount owed in the present and the amount that has to be paid in the future to settle the debt.

Chapter 12. Market Power

a. Discount
b. Reliability theory
c. Reinsurance
d. Certified Risk Manager

28. A _____ rocket is a rocket that uses two or more stages, each of which contains its own engines and propellant. A tandem or serial stage is mounted on top of another stage; a parallel stage is attached alongside another stage. The result is effectively two or more rockets stacked on top of or attached next to each other.

a. Multistage
b. 100-year flood
c. 130-30 fund
d. 1921 recession

29. _____ is a model of competition used in economics it is a model of price competition between duopoly firms which results in each charging the price that would be charged under perfect competition, known as marginal cost pricing.

The model has the following assumptions:

- There are at least two firms producing homogeneous products;
- Firms do not cooperate;
- Firms have the same marginal cost (MC);
- Marginal cost is constant;
- Demand is linear;
- Firms compete in price, and choose their respective prices simultaneously;
- There is strategic behaviour by both firms;
- Both firms compete solely on price and then supply the quantity demanded;
- Consumers buy everything from the cheaper firm or half at each, if the price is equal.

Competing in price means that firms can easily change the quantity they supply, but once they have chosen a certain price, it is very hard, if not impossible, to change it. Some examples of firms that might operate in this way are bars, shops or other companies that publish non-negotiable prices.

- MC = Marginal cost
- p_1 = firm 1e;s price level
- p_2 = firm 2e;s price level
- p^M = monopoly price level

- Firm 1s optimum price depends on where it believes firm 2 will set its prices. Pricing just below the other firm will obtain full market demand , while maximizing profits.

a. Guns versus butter model
b. Bertrand competition
c. Vicarious problem solving
d. Goodwin model

30. A _____ provision refers to any program which seeks to provide a minimum level of income, service or other support for many marginalized groups such as the poor, elderly, and disabled people. _____ programs are undertaken by governments as well as non-governmental organizations (NGOs.) _____ payments and services are typically provided at the expense of taxpayers generally, funded by benefactors, or by compulsory enrollment of the poor themselves.

Chapter 12. Market Power

a. 1921 recession
b. 100-year flood
c. 130-30 fund
d. Social welfare

31. _____ is a term used to described a tendency or preference towards a particular perspective, ideology or result, especially when the tendency interferes with the ability to be impartial, unprejudiced, or objective. The term _____ed is used to describe an action, judgment, or other outcome influenced by a prejudged perspective. It is also used to refer to a person or body of people whose actions or judgments exhibit _____.
 a. 130-30 fund
 b. 1921 recession
 c. Bias
 d. 100-year flood

32. In economics, a _____ is a market served by only one firm, but with mandated 'competitive' pricing, so as to second the monopoly held by said firm on said market. Its fundamental feature is low barriers to entry and exit; a perfectly _____ would have no barriers to entry or exit. _____s are characterised by 'hit and run' entry.
 a. Contestable market
 b. Perfect market
 c. Horizontal market
 d. Market mechanism

33. _____ is a decision rule used in decision theory, game theory, statistics and philosophy for minimizing the maximum possible loss. Alternatively, it can be thought of as maximizing the minimum gain (maximin.) It started from two-player zero-sum game theory, covering both the cases where players take alternate moves and those where they make simultaneous moves.
 a. 130-30 fund
 b. Design Impact Measures
 c. 100-year flood
 d. Minimax

34. In business, _____ refers to any action taken by an existing business in a particular market that discourages potential entrants from entering into competition in that market. Such actions, or barriers to entry, can include hostile takeovers, product differentiation through heavy spending on new product development, capacity expansion to achieve lower unit costs, and predatory pricing. These actions are sometimes deemed anti-competitive and could be subject to various competition laws.
 a. Strategic entry deterrence
 b. Non-price competition
 c. Moral victory
 d. Price-fixing

35. The _____ describes a firm's market power. It is defined by:

$$L = \frac{P - MC}{P}$$

where P is the market price set by the firm and MC is the firm's marginal cost. The index ranges from a high of 1 to a low of 0, with higher numbers implying greater market power.

 a. Break even analysis
 b. Two-part tariff
 c. Discounts and allowances
 d. Lerner index

36. _____ theory, pioneered by American economist Paul Samuelson, is a method by which it is possible to discern the best possible option on the basis of consumer behavior. Essentially, this means that the preferences of consumers can be revealed by their purchasing habits. _____ theory came about because the theories of consumer demand were based on a diminishing marginal rate of substitution (MRS.)

Chapter 12. Market Power

a. Marginal rate of substitution
b. Joint demand
c. Rational addiction
d. Revealed preference

37. The _____ is a measure of the size of firms in relation to the industry and an indicator of the amount of competition among them. Named after economists Orris C. Herfindahl and Albert O. Hirschman, it is an economic concept, widely applied in competition law, antitrust and also technology management. It is defined as the sum of the squares of the market shares of the 50 largest firms within the industry, where the market shares are expressed as percentages.

a. Reduced form
b. Vector autoregression
c. Panel data
d. Herfindahl index

38. _____ is a term used in economics to describe how an economic quantity is related to economic fluctuations. It is the opposite of procyclical. However, it has more than one meaning.

a. Law of comparative advantage
b. Price revolution
c. Countercyclical
d. Mathematical economics

Chapter 13. Adverse Selection, Signaling, and Screening

1. _____ is an important concept in economics with broad applications in game theory, engineering and the social sciences. The term is named after Vilfredo Pareto, an Italian economist who used the concept in his studies of economic efficiency and income distribution. Informally, pareto efficient situations are those in which any change to make any person better off would make someone else worse off.
   a. Perfect rationality
   b. Matching pennies
   c. Lump of labour
   d. Pareto efficiency

2. _____s is the social science that studies the production, distribution, and consumption of goods and services. The term _____s comes from the Ancient Greek οἰκονομία from οἶκος (oikos, 'house') + νόμος (nomos, 'custom' or 'law'), hence 'rules of the house(hold)'. Current _____ models developed out of the broader field of political economy in the late 19th century, owing to a desire to use an empirical approach more akin to the physical sciences.
   a. Energy economics
   b. Opportunity cost
   c. Inflation
   d. Economic

3. _____ is a branch of economics that uses microeconomic techniques to simultaneously determine allocative efficiency within an economy and the income distribution associated with it. It analyzes social welfare, however measured, in terms of economic activities of the individuals that comprise the theoretical society considered. As such, individuals, with associated economic activities, are the basic units for aggregating to social welfare, whether of a group, a community, or a society, and there is no 'social welfare' apart from the 'welfare' associated with its individual units.
   a. Tobit model
   b. General equilibrium
   c. Welfare economics
   d. Law of increasing costs

4. _____, anti-selection insurance, statistics, and risk management. It refers to a market process in which 'bad' results occur when buyers and sellers have asymmetric information (i.e. access to different information): the 'bad' products or customers are more likely to be selected. A bank that sets one price for all its checking account customers runs the risk of being adversely selected against by its low-balance, high-activity (and hence least profitable) customers.
   a. AD-IA Model
   b. ACEA agreement
   c. Adverse selection
   d. ACCRA Cost of Living Index

5. Competitive market equilibrium is the traditional concept of economic equilibrium, appropriate for the analysis of commodity markets with flexible prices and many traders, and serving as the benchmark of efficiency in economic analysis. It relies crucially on the assumption of a competitive environment where each trader decides upon a quantity that is so small compared to the total quantity traded in the market that their individual transactions have no influence on the prices. Competitive markets are an ideal, a standard that other market structures are evaluated by.

A _____ consists of a vector of prices and an allocation such that given the prices, each trader by maximizing his objective function (profit, preferences) subject to his technological possibilities and resource constraints plans to trade into his part of the proposed allocation, and such that the prices make all net trades compatible with one another ('clear the market') by equating aggregate supply and demand for the commodities which are traded.

   a. Competitive equilibrium
   b. Market system
   c. Partial equilibrium
   d. Product-Market Growth Matrix

6. _____ is an assumption used in many contemporary macroeconomic models, and also in other areas of contemporary economics and game theory and in other applications of rational choice theory.

Since most macroeconomic models today study decisions over many periods, the expectations of workers, consumers, and firms about future economic conditions are an essential part of the model. How to model these expectations has long been controversial, and it is well known that the macroeconomic predictions of the model may differ depending on the assumptions made about expectations

   a. Potential output
   b. Balanced-growth equilibrium
   c. Rational expectations
   d. Minimum wage

7. In economics, an _____ is a way of representing various distributions of resources. Edgeworth made his presentation in his famous book, Mathematical Psychics: An essay on the application of mathematics to the moral sciences, 1881. Edgeworth's original two axis depiction was developed into the now familiar box diagram by Pareto in 1906 and was popularized in a later exposition by Bowley.

   a. ACCRA Cost of Living Index
   b. International Social Security Association
   c. Equivalent variation
   d. Edgeworth box

8. _____ in economics refers to metrics and measures of output from production processes, per unit of input. Labor _____, for example, is typically measured as a ratio of output per labor-hour, an input. _____ may be conceived of as a metrics of the technical or engineering efficiency of production.

   a. Fordism
   b. Piece work
   c. Production-possibility frontier
   d. Productivity

9. _____ is the electoral problem resulting from competition between two or more candidates or political parties from the same or approximate location in the political ideological spectrum or space against an opposing candidate or political party from the other side of the political ideological spectrum or space. The resulting fragmentation of political support may result in electoral defeat. _____s, and thus political calculations attempting to avoid them, appear most frequently in elections involving executives and representatives from single member districts.

   a. 100-year flood
   b. 1921 recession
   c. 130-30 fund
   d. Coordination failure

10. In labor economics, the _____ is the lowest wage rate at which a worker would be willing to accept a particular type of job. A job offer involving the same type of work and the same working conditions, but at a lower wage rate, would be rejected by the worker.

An individual's _____ may change over time depending on a number of factors, like changes in the individual's overall wealth, changes in marital status or living arrangements, length of unemployment, and health and disability issues.

   a. Reservation wage
   b. Dematerialization
   c. Minsky moment
   d. Stylized fact

11. A _____ provision refers to any program which seeks to provide a minimum level of income, service or other support for many marginalized groups such as the poor, elderly, and disabled people. _____ programs are undertaken by governments as well as non-governmental organizations (NGOs.) _____ payments and services are typically provided at the expense of taxpayers generally, funded by benefactors, or by compulsory enrollment of the poor themselves.

Chapter 13. Adverse Selection, Signaling, and Screening

a. 1921 recession
c. Social welfare
b. 130-30 fund
d. 100-year flood

12. In economics, a _____ is a real-valued function that ranks conceivable social states (alternative complete descriptions of the society) from lowest to highest. Inputs of the function include any variables considered to affect welfare of the society (Sen, 1970, p. 33.)
   a. Gini coefficient
   c. Contract curve
   b. Frisch elasticity of labor supply
   d. Social welfare function

13. The term _____ is a neo-Latin word meaning 'before the event'. _____ is used most commonly in the commercial world, where results of a particular action, or series of actions, are forecast in advance. The opposite of _____ is ex-post .
   a. ACEA agreement
   c. ACCRA Cost of Living Index
   b. AD-IA Model
   d. Ex-ante

14. In economics and sociology, an _____ is any factor (financial or non-financial) that enables or motivates a particular course of action, or counts as a reason for preferring one choice to the alternatives. It is an expectation that encourages people to behave in a certain way. Since human beings are purposeful creatures, the study of _____ structures is central to the study of all economic activity (both in terms of individual decision-making and in terms of co-operation and competition within a larger institutional structure.)
   a. Epstein-Zin preferences
   c. Isocost
   b. Economic reform
   d. Incentive

15. _____ refers to methods in probability and statistics named after the Reverend Thomas Bayes (ca. 1702-1761), in particular methods related to:

- the degree-of-belief interpretation of probability, as opposed to frequency or proportion or propensity interpretations; or
- Bayes' theorem on conditional probability.

Chapter 13. Adverse Selection, Signaling, and Screening

These methods include:

- Bayes estimator
- Bayes factor
- _____ average
- _____ spam filtering
- _____ game
- _____ inference
- _____ information criterion
- _____ multivariate linear regression
    - _____ linear regression, a special case
- _____ model comparison
- _____ network
- _____ probability
- Empirical Bayes method
- Naive Bayes classifier

_____ also refers to the application of this probability theory to the functioning of the brain

- _____ brain

a. Bayesian
c. Fiscal

b. Technocracy
d. Freedom Park

Chapter 13. Adverse Selection, Signaling, and Screening 75

16. A _____ is:

- Rewrite _____, in generative grammar and computer science
- Standardization, a formal and widely-accepted statement, fact, definition, or qualification
- Operation, a determinate _____ for performing a mathematical operation and obtaining a certain result (Mathematics, Logic)
    - Unary operation
    - Binary operation
- _____ of inference, a function from sets of formulae to formulae (Mathematics, Logic)
- _____ of thumb, principle with broad application that is not intended to be strictly accurate or reliable for every situation. Also often simply referred to as a _____
- Moral, an atomic element of a moral code for guiding choices in human behavior
- Heuristic, a quantized '_____' which shows a tendency or probability for successful function
- A regulation, as in sports
- A Production _____, as in computer science
- Procedural law, a _____ set governing the application of laws to cases
    - A law, which may informally be called a '_____'
    - A court ruling, a decision by a court
- In the U.S. Government, a regulation mandated by Congress, but written or expanded upon by the Executive Branch.
- Norm (sociology), an informal but widely accepted _____, concept, truth, definition, or qualification (social norms, legal norms, coding norms)
- Norm (philosophy), a kind of sentence or a reason to act, feel or believe
- 'Rulership' is the concept of governance by a government:
    - Military _____, governance by a military body
    - Monastic _____, a collection of precepts that guides the life of monks or nuns in a religious order where the superior holds the place of Christ
- Slide _____

- '_____,' a song by Ayumi Hamasaki
- '_____,' a song by rapper Nas
- '_____s,' an album by the band The Whitest Boy Alive
- _____s: Pyaar Ka Superhit Formula, a 2003 Bollywood film
- ruler, an instrument for measuring lengths
- _____, a component of an astrolabe, circumferator or similar instrument
- The _____s, a bestselling self-help book
- _____ Project (Run Up-to-date Linux Everywhere), a project that aims to use up-to-date Linux software on old PCs
- _____ engine, a software system that helps managing business _____s
- Ja _____, a hip hop artist
    - R.U.L.E., a 2005 greatest hits album by rapper Ja _____
- '_____s,' a KMFDM song

a. Procter ' Gamble
c. Technocracy
b. Demand
d. Rule

Chapter 13. Adverse Selection, Signaling, and Screening

17. _____, in law and economics, is a form of risk management primarily used to hedge against the risk of a contingent loss. _____ is defined as the equitable transfer of the risk of a loss, from one entity to another, in exchange for a premium, and can be thought of as a guaranteed small loss to prevent a large, possibly devastating loss. An insurer is a company selling the _____; an insured or policyholder is the person or entity buying the _____.
    a. ACEA agreement
    b. ACCRA Cost of Living Index
    c. AD-IA Model
    d. Insurance

18. _____ is a refinement of Nash Equilibrium for extensive form games due to David M. Kreps and Robert Wilson. A _____ specifies not only a strategy for each of the players but also a belief for each of the players. A belief gives, for each information set of the game belonging to the player, a probability distribution on the nodes in the information set.
    a. Markov strategy
    b. Pursuit-evasion
    c. Sequential equilibrium
    d. Matching pennies

19. _____ are dynamic games with two players, the sender (S) and the receiver (R.) The sender has a certain type, t, which is given by nature. The sender observes his own type while the receiver does not know the type of the sender.
    a. Quasi-perfect equilibrium
    b. Complete information
    c. Signalling games
    d. Pareto efficiency

20. In game theory, _____ is a solution concept of a game involving two or more players, in which each player is assumed to know the equilibrium strategies of the other players, and no player has anything to gain by changing only his or her own strategy unilaterally. If each player has chosen a strategy and no player can benefit by changing his or her strategy while the other players keep theirs unchanged, then the current set of strategy choices and the corresponding payoffs constitute a _____.

    Stated simply, Amy and Bill are in _____ if Amy is making the best decision she can, taking into account Bill's decision, and Bill is making the best decision he can, taking into account Amy's decision.

    a. Linear production game
    b. Proper equilibrium
    c. Lump of labour
    d. Nash equilibrium

21. _____ in economics and business is the result of an exchange and from that trade we assign a numerical monetary value to a good, service or asset. If Alice trades Bob 4 apples for an orange, the _____ of an orange is 4 apples. Inversely, the _____ of an apple is 1/4 oranges.
    a. Premium pricing
    b. Price war
    c. Price book
    d. Price

22. An _____ is a person who has possession of an enterprise and assumes significant accountability for the inherent risks and the outcome. It is an ambitious leader who combines land, labor, and capital to create and market new goods or services. The term is a loanword from French and was first defined by the Irish economist Richard Cantillon.
    a. ACCRA Cost of Living Index
    b. Expansionary policies
    c. Entrepreneur
    d. ACEA agreement

Chapter 14. The Principal-Agent Problem

1. _____ is the prospect that a party insulated from risk may behave differently from the way it would behave if it were fully exposed to the risk. In insurance, _____ that occurs without conscious or malicious action is called morale hazard.

   _____ is related to information asymmetry, a situation in which one party in a transaction has more information than another.

   a. 1921 recession
   b. 100-year flood
   c. 130-30 fund
   d. Moral hazard

2. In economics and sociology, an _____ is any factor (financial or non-financial) that enables or motivates a particular course of action, or counts as a reason for preferring one choice to the alternatives. It is an expectation that encourages people to behave in a certain way. Since human beings are purposeful creatures, the study of _____ structures is central to the study of all economic activity (both in terms of individual decision-making and in terms of co-operation and competition within a larger institutional structure.)
   a. Epstein-Zin preferences
   b. Incentive
   c. Isocost
   d. Economic reform

3. In probability theory, a probability _____ of a random variable is a function which describes the density of probability at each point in the sample space. The probability of a random variable falling within a given set is given by the integral of its density over the set.

   A probability _____ is most commonly associated with continuous univariate distributions.

   a. Graphical model
   b. Density function
   c. Memorylessness
   d. Markov blanket

4. In economics, _____ is a measure of the relative satisfaction from consumption of various goods and services. Given this measure, one may speak meaningfully of increasing or decreasing _____, and thereby explain economic behavior in terms of attempts to increase one's _____. For illustrative purposes, changes in _____ are sometimes expressed in units called utils.
   a. Utility function
   b. Ordinal utility
   c. Expected utility hypothesis
   d. Utility

5. While preferences are the conventional foundation of microeconomics, it is often convenient to represent preferences with a _____ and reason indirectly about preferences with _____s. Let X be the consumption set, the set of all mutually-exclusive packages the consumer could conceivably consume (such as an indifference curve map without the indifference curves.) The consumer's _____ $u : X \to \mathbf{R}$ ranks each package in the consumption set.
   a. Utility function
   b. Utility
   c. Expected utility hypothesis
   d. Ordinal utility

6. _____ is a concept in economics, finance, and psychology related to the behaviour of consumers and investors under uncertainty. _____ is the reluctance of a person to accept a bargain with an uncertain payoff rather than another bargain with a more certain, but possibly lower, expected payoff. For example, a risk-averse investor might choose to put his or her money into a bank account with a low but guaranteed interest rate, rather than into a stock that is likely to have high returns, but also has a chance of becoming worthless.

Chapter 14. The Principal-Agent Problem

a. Risk theory
b. Reinsurance
c. Compound annual growth rate
d. Risk aversion

7. _____ is a property of a family of probability distributions described by their probability density functions (PDFs.)

A family of density functions $\{f_\theta(x)\}_{\theta \in \Theta}$ indexed by a parameter θ taking values in a set Θ is said to have the monotone likelihood ratio (MLR) in a statistic T(X) if for any two parameter values $\theta_1 < \theta_2$, the ratio $f_{\theta_2}(x)/f_{\theta_1}(x)$ is a non-decreasing function of T(X).

The _____ can be used in hypothesis tests, primarily when dealing with composite null hypotheses.

a. Cash taxes
b. Demographic marketers
c. Basis of futures
d. Monotone likelihood ratio property

8. A _____ is an expression that compares quantities relative to each other. The most common examples involve two quantities, but any number of quantities can be compared. _____s are represented mathematically by separating each quantity with a colon, for example the _____ 2:3, which is read as the _____ 'two to three'.
a. 130-30 fund
b. 100-year flood
c. Y-intercept
d. Ratio

9. The _____ of economics can be stated as, 'To any Bayesian Nash equilibrium of a game of incomplete information, there corresponds an associated revelation mechanism that has an equilibrium where the players truthfully report their types.'

For dominant strategies, instead of Bayesian equilibrium, the _____ was introduced by Gibbard (1973.) Later this principle was extended to the broader solution concept of Bayesian equilibrium by Dasgupta, Hammond and Maskin (1979), Holmstrom (1977), and Myerson (1979.)

The _____ is useful in game theory, Mechanism design, social welfare and auctions.

a. Revelation principle
b. X-inefficiency
c. X-efficiency
d. 100-year flood

10. In mechanism design, a process is said to be incentive compatible if all of the participants fare best when they truthfully reveal any private information asked for by the mechanism . As an illustration, voting systems which create incentives to vote dishonestly lack the property of _____. In the absence of dummy bidders or collusion, a second price auction is an example of mechanism that is incentive compatible.
a. ACEA agreement
b. ACCRA Cost of Living Index
c. AD-IA Model
d. Incentive compatibility

11. _____ in economics and business is the result of an exchange and from that trade we assign a numerical monetary value to a good, service or asset. If Alice trades Bob 4 apples for an orange, the _____ of an orange is 4 apples. Inversely, the _____ of an apple is 1/4 oranges.

Chapter 14. The Principal-Agent Problem

a. Price
b. Premium pricing
c. Price book
d. Price war

12. _____ exists when sales of identical goods or services are transacted at different prices from the same provider. In a theoretical market with perfect information, no transaction costs or prohibition on secondary exchange (or re-selling) to prevent arbitrage, _____ can only be a feature of monopoly and oligopoly markets, where market power can be exercised. Otherwise, the moment the seller tries to sell the same good at different prices, the buyer at the lower price can arbitrage by selling to the consumer buying at the higher price but with a tiny discount.
    a. Loss leader
    b. Lerner Index
    c. Transfer pricing
    d. Price discrimination

13. _____, in law and economics, is a form of risk management primarily used to hedge against the risk of a contingent loss. _____ is defined as the equitable transfer of the risk of a loss, from one entity to another, in exchange for a premium, and can be thought of as a guaranteed small loss to prevent a large, possibly devastating loss. An insurer is a company selling the _____; an insured or policyholder is the person or entity buying the _____.
    a. Insurance
    b. AD-IA Model
    c. ACCRA Cost of Living Index
    d. ACEA agreement

14. _____ theory is a branch of theoretical economics. It seeks to explain the behavior of supply, demand and prices in a whole economy with several or many markets. It is often assumed that agents are price takers and in that setting two common notions of equilibrium exist: Walrasian (or competitive) equilibrium, and its generalization; a price equilibrium with transfers.
    a. Rational choice theory
    b. New Keynesian economics
    c. Human capital
    d. General equilibrium

15. _____ is a branch of theoretical economics. It seeks to explain the behavior of supply, demand and prices in a whole economy with several or many markets. It is often assumed that agents are price takers and in that setting two common notions of equilibrium exist: Walrasian (or competitive) equilibrium, and its generalization; a price equilibrium with transfers.
    a. Public economics
    b. Monetary economics
    c. Leading indicators
    d. General equilibrium theory

Chapter 15. General Equilibrium Theory: Some Examples

1. In economics, an _____ is a way of representing various distributions of resources. Edgeworth made his presentation in his famous book, Mathematical Psychics: An essay on the application of mathematics to the moral sciences, 1881. Edgeworth's original two axis depiction was developed into the now familiar box diagram by Pareto in 1906 and was popularized in a later exposition by Bowley.
   a. Equivalent variation
   b. ACCRA Cost of Living Index
   c. International Social Security Association
   d. Edgeworth box

2. _____ theory is a branch of theoretical economics. It seeks to explain the behavior of supply, demand and prices in a whole economy with several or many markets. It is often assumed that agents are price takers and in that setting two common notions of equilibrium exist: Walrasian (or competitive) equilibrium, and its generalization; a price equilibrium with transfers.
   a. General equilibrium
   b. Human capital
   c. New Keynesian economics
   d. Rational choice theory

3. _____ is a branch of theoretical economics. It seeks to explain the behavior of supply, demand and prices in a whole economy with several or many markets. It is often assumed that agents are price takers and in that setting two common notions of equilibrium exist: Walrasian (or competitive) equilibrium, and its generalization; a price equilibrium with transfers.
   a. Leading indicators
   b. Monetary economics
   c. General equilibrium theory
   d. Public economics

4. A _____ includes all possible consumption bundles that someone can afford given the prices of goods and the person's income level. The _____ is bounded above by the budget line.
   a. Budget set
   b. Budget surplus
   c. 130-30 fund
   d. 100-year flood

5. Economics:

   - _____, the desire to own something and the ability to pay for it
   - _____ curve, a graphic representation of a _____ schedule
   - _____ deposit, the money in checking accounts
   - _____ pull theory, the theory that inflation occurs when _____ for goods and services exceeds existing supplies
   - _____ schedule, a table that lists the quantity of a good a person will buy it each different price
   - _____ side economics, the school of economics at believes government spending and tax cuts open economy by raising _____

   a. Variability
   b. Production
   c. Demand
   d. McKesson ' Robbins scandal

6. In economics and particularly in international trade, an _____ shows the quantity of one type of product that an agent will export ('offer') for each quantity of another type of product that it imports. The _____ was first derived by English economists Edgeworth and Marshall to help explain international trade.

The _____ is derived from the country's PPF.

a. ACEA agreement
b. AD-IA Model
c. Offer curve
d. ACCRA Cost of Living Index

7. In economics, _____ is when quantity demanded is more than quantity supplied. See Economic shortage.
   a. AD-IA Model
   b. Excess demand
   c. ACEA agreement
   d. ACCRA Cost of Living Index

8. In economics, _____ is when quantity supplied is more than quantity demanded. .
   a. Illicit financial flows
   b. Effective unemployment rate
   c. Economic Value Creation
   d. Excess supply

9. In economics, the _____ functional form of production functions is widely used to represent the relationship of an output to inputs. It was proposed by Knut Wicksell (1851-1926), and tested against statistical evidence by Charles Cobb and Paul Douglas in 1900-1928.

For production, the function is

$$Y = AL^{\alpha}K^{\beta},$$

where:

- Y = total production (the monetary value of all goods produced in a year)
- L = labor input
- K = capital input
- A = total factor productivity
- α and β are the output elasticities of labor and capital, respectively. These values are constants determined by available technology.

Output elasticity measures the responsiveness of output to a change in levels of either labor or capital used in production, ceteris paribus. For example if α = 0.15, a 1% increase in labor would lead to approximately a 0.15% increase in output.

a. Growth accounting
b. Social savings
c. Cobb-Douglas
d. Demand-pull theory

10. In economics, _____ is a measure of the relative satisfaction from consumption of various goods and services. Given this measure, one may speak meaningfully of increasing or decreasing _____, and thereby explain economic behavior in terms of attempts to increase one's _____. For illustrative purposes, changes in _____ are sometimes expressed in units called utils.
    a. Utility
    b. Utility function
    c. Expected utility hypothesis
    d. Ordinal utility

Chapter 15. General Equilibrium Theory: Some Examples

11. While preferences are the conventional foundation of microeconomics, it is often convenient to represent preferences with a _____ and reason indirectly about preferences with _____s. Let X be the consumption set, the set of all mutually-exclusive packages the consumer could conceivably consume (such as an indifference curve map without the indifference curves.) The consumer's _____ $u : X \to \mathbf{R}$ ranks each package in the consumption set.
   a. Ordinal utility
   b. Expected utility hypothesis
   c. Utility
   d. Utility function

12. _____ in economics and business is the result of an exchange and from that trade we assign a numerical monetary value to a good, service or asset. If Alice trades Bob 4 apples for an orange, the _____ of an orange is 4 apples. Inversely, the _____ of an apple is 1/4 oranges.
   a. Premium pricing
   b. Price war
   c. Price book
   d. Price

13. In economics, _____ is the transfer of income, wealth or property from some individuals to others.

One premise of _____ is that money should be distributed to benefit the poorer members of society, and that the rich have an obligation to assist the poor, thus creating a more financially egalitarian society. Another argument is that the rich exploit the poor or otherwise gain unfair benefits.

   a. 100-year flood
   b. 130-30 fund
   c. 1921 recession
   d. Redistribution

14. _____ is an important concept in economics with broad applications in game theory, engineering and the social sciences. The term is named after Vilfredo Pareto, an Italian economist who used the concept in his studies of economic efficiency and income distribution. Informally, pareto efficient situations are those in which any change to make any person better off would make someone else worse off.
   a. Pareto efficiency
   b. Matching pennies
   c. Perfect rationality
   d. Lump of labour

15. Given some endowment in an Edgeworth box, the _____ is the individually rational subset of the Pareto set. In other words, it is the set of Pareto efficient allocations in an economy. Also, any Walrasian equilibrium lies in the _____ of the Pareto set.
   a. Contract curve
   b. Missing market
   c. Hidden Welfare State
   d. Social welfare function

16. In microeconomics in general, and game theory in particular, the _____ is the set of all Pareto-efficient outcomes.
   a. Screening game
   b. Stable marriage problem
   c. Self-confirming equilibrium
   d. Pareto set

17. _____ was a survey conducted by the U.S. Department of Justice to gauge the prevalence of alcohol and illegal drug use among prior arrestees. It was a reformulation of the prior Drug Use Forecasting (DUF) program, focused on five drugs in particular: cocaine, marijuana, methamphetamine, opiates, and PCP.

Participants were randomly selected from arrest records in major metropolitan areas; because no personally identifying information is taken from each record chosen, the resulting data can be correlated to arrest rates, but not to the total population of persons charged.

Chapter 15. General Equilibrium Theory: Some Examples

a. Arrestee Drug Abuse Monitoring
b. AD-IA Model
c. ACCRA Cost of Living Index
d. ACEA agreement

18. In economics, the _____ is the term economists use to describe the self-regulating nature of the marketplace. The _____ is a metaphor coined by the economist Adam Smith in The Wealth of Nations.

Adam Smith mentions the metaphor in Book IV of The Wealth of Nations, arguing that people in any society will certainly employ their capital in foreign trading only if the profits available by that method far exceed those available locally, and that in such a case it is better for society as a whole if they so did.

a. ACCRA Cost of Living Index
b. AD-IA Model
c. ACEA agreement
d. Invisible hand

19. _____ was a Scottish moral philosopher and a pioneer of political economy. One of the key figures of the Scottish Enlightenment, Smith is the author of The Theory of Moral Sentiments and An Inquiry into the Nature and Causes of the Wealth of Nations. The latter, usually abbreviated as The Wealth of Nations, is considered his magnum opus and the first modern work of economics.

a. Adolf Hitler
b. Adolph Fischer
c. Alan Greenspan
d. Adam Smith

20. _____s is the social science that studies the production, distribution, and consumption of goods and services. The term _____s comes from the Ancient Greek oá¼°κονομῖα from oá¼¶κος (oikos, 'house') + vÏŒμος (nomos, 'custom' or 'law'), hence 'rules of the house(hold)'. Current _____ models developed out of the broader field of political economy in the late 19th century, owing to a desire to use an empirical approach more akin to the physical sciences.

a. Energy economics
b. Inflation
c. Opportunity cost
d. Economic

21. _____ is a branch of economics that uses microeconomic techniques to simultaneously determine allocative efficiency within an economy and the income distribution associated with it. It analyzes social welfare, however measured, in terms of economic activities of the individuals that comprise the theoretical society considered. As such, individuals, with associated economic activities, are the basic units for aggregating to social welfare, whether of a group, a community, or a society, and there is no 'social welfare' apart from the 'welfare' associated with its individual units.

a. Welfare economics
b. Tobit model
c. General equilibrium
d. Law of increasing costs

22. A _____ represents the combinations of goods and services that a consumer can purchase given current prices and his income. Consumer theory uses the concepts of a _____ and a preference map to analyze consumer choices. Both concepts have a ready graphical representation in the two-good case.

a. Quality bias
b. Budget constraint
c. Joint demand
d. Revealed preference

23. Competitive market equilibrium is the traditional concept of economic equilibrium, appropriate for the analysis of commodity markets with flexible prices and many traders, and serving as the benchmark of efficiency in economic analysis. It relies crucially on the assumption of a competitive environment where each trader decides upon a quantity that is so small compared to the total quantity traded in the market that their individual transactions have no influence on the prices.Competitive markets are an ideal, a standard that other market structures are evaluated by.

Chapter 15. General Equilibrium Theory: Some Examples

A _____ consists of a vector of prices and an allocation such that given the prices, each trader by maximizing his objective function (profit, preferences) subject to his technological possibilities and resource constraints plans to trade into his part of the proposed allocation, and such that the prices make all net trades compatible with one another ('clear the market') by equating aggregate supply and demand for the commodities which are traded.

a. Partial equilibrium
b. Product-Market Growth Matrix
c. Market system
d. Competitive equilibrium

24. In microeconomics, _____ is quite simply the conversion of inputs into outputs. It is an economic process that uses resources to create a good or service that is suitable for exchange. This can include manufacturing, storing, shipping, and packaging.
a. Red Guards
b. Production
c. MET
d. Solved

25. In economics a country's _____ is commonly understood as the amount of land, labor, capital, and entrepreneurship that a country possesses and can exploit for manufacturing. Countries with a large endowment of resources tend to be more prosperous than those with a small endowment, all other things being equal. The development of sound institutions to access and equitably distribute these resources, however, is necessary in order for a country to obtain the greatest benefit from its _____.

a. Foreign Affiliate Trade Statistics
b. Factor endowment
c. Dutch disease
d. Price scissors

26. _____ are the prices that the factors of production of a finished item attract.

There has been some economic debate as to what determines these prices. Classical and Marxist economists argued that the _____ decided the value of a product and so value was intrinsic within the product.

a. Marginal product
b. Productivity model
c. Marginal product of labor
d. Factor prices

27. In economics, a _____ is a function that specifies the output of a firm, an industry, or an entire economy for all combinations of inputs. A meta-_____ compares the practice of the existing entities converting inputs X into output y to determine the most efficient practice _____ of the existing entities, whether the most efficient feasible practice production or the most efficient actual practice production. In either case, the maximum output of a technologically-determined production process is a mathematical function of input factors of production.
a. Production function
b. Post-Fordism
c. Short-run
d. Constant elasticity of substitution

28. The _____ is a basic theorem in trade theory. It describes a relation between the relative prices of output goods and relative factor rewards, specifically, real wages and real returns to capital.

The theorem states that -- under some economic assumptions (constant returns, perfect competition) -- a rise in the relative price of a good will lead to a rise in the return to that factor which is used most intensively in the production of the good, and conversely, to a fall in the return to the other factor.

Chapter 15. General Equilibrium Theory: Some Examples

a. Heckscher-Ohlin theorem
c. 100-year flood
b. Stolper-Samuelson theorem
d. No-trade theorem

29. A _____ is an expression that compares quantities relative to each other. The most common examples involve two quantities, but any number of quantities can be compared. _____s are represented mathematically by separating each quantity with a colon, for example the _____ 2:3, which is read as the _____ 'two to three'.
   a. Ratio
   c. 130-30 fund
   b. 100-year flood
   d. Y-intercept

30. A _____ is a type of economic equilibrium, where the clearance on the market of some specific goods is obtained independently from prices and quantities demanded and supplied in other markets. In other words, the prices of all substitutes and complements, as well as income levels of consumers are constant. Here the dynamic process is that prices adjust until supply equals demand.
   a. Market depth
   c. Horizontal market
   b. Market system
   d. Partial equilibrium

31. To _____ is to impose a financial charge or other levy upon a taxpayer by a state or the functional equivalent of a state.

    _____es are also imposed by many subnational entities. _____es consist of direct _____ or indirect _____, and may be paid in money or as its labour equivalent (often but not always unpaid.)

   a. Tax
   c. 1921 recession
   b. 100-year flood
   d. 130-30 fund

32. In economics, _____ is the analysis of the effect of a particular tax on the distribution of economic welfare. _____ is said to 'fall' upon the group that, at the end of the day, bears the burden of the tax. The key concept is that the _____ or tax burden does not depend on where the revenue is collected, but on the price elasticity of demand and price elasticity of supply.
   a. Tax incidence
   c. 1921 recession
   b. 130-30 fund
   d. 100-year flood

33. The _____ is the apparent contradiction that although water is on the whole more useful, in terms of survival, than diamonds, diamonds command a higher price in the market. The economist Adam Smith is often considered to be the classic presenter of this paradox. Nicolaus Copernicus, John Locke, John Law and others had previously tried to explain the disparity.
   a. 100-year flood
   c. 130-30 fund
   b. St. Petersburg paradox
   d. Paradox of value

34. The _____ is one of the four critical theorems of the Heckscher-Ohlin model. It states: 'A capital-abundant country will export the capital-intensive good, while the labor-abundant country will export the labor-intensive good.'

The critical assumption of the Heckscher-Ohlin model is that the two countries are identical, except for the difference in resource endowments. This also implies that the aggregate preferences are the same.

a. Stolper-Samuelson theorem
b. No-trade theorem
c. 100-year flood
d. Heckscher-Ohlin theorem

Chapter 16. Equilibrium and Its Basic Welfare Properties

1. _____ is an important concept in economics with broad applications in game theory, engineering and the social sciences. The term is named after Vilfredo Pareto, an Italian economist who used the concept in his studies of economic efficiency and income distribution. Informally, pareto efficient situations are those in which any change to make any person better off would make someone else worse off.

   a. Matching pennies
   b. Perfect rationality
   c. Pareto efficiency
   d. Lump of labour

2. _____ in economics and business is the result of an exchange and from that trade we assign a numerical monetary value to a good, service or asset. If Alice trades Bob 4 apples for an orange, the _____ of an orange is 4 apples. Inversely, the _____ of an apple is 1/4 oranges.

   a. Price book
   b. Premium pricing
   c. Price
   d. Price war

3. In economics, _____ is the process by which a firm determines the price and output level that returns the greatest profit. There are several approaches to this problem. The total revenue--total cost method relies on the fact that profit equals revenue minus cost, and the marginal revenue--marginal cost method is based on the fact that total profit in a perfectly competitive market reaches its maximum point where marginal revenue equals marginal cost.

   a. Profit maximization
   b. Profit margin
   c. 100-year flood
   d. Normal profit

4. _____ was a survey conducted by the U.S. Department of Justice to gauge the prevalence of alcohol and illegal drug use among prior arrestees. It was a reformulation of the prior Drug Use Forecasting (DUF) program, focused on five drugs in particular: cocaine, marijuana, methamphetamine, opiates, and PCP.

   Participants were randomly selected from arrest records in major metropolitan areas; because no personally identifying information is taken from each record chosen, the resulting data can be correlated to arrest rates, but not to the total population of persons charged.

   a. Arrestee Drug Abuse Monitoring
   b. AD-IA Model
   c. ACCRA Cost of Living Index
   d. ACEA agreement

5. In economics, the _____ is the term economists use to describe the self-regulating nature of the marketplace. The _____ is a metaphor coined by the economist Adam Smith in The Wealth of Nations.

   Adam Smith mentions the metaphor in Book IV of The Wealth of Nations, arguing that people in any society will certainly employ their capital in foreign trading only if the profits available by that method far exceed those available locally, and that in such a case it is better for society as a whole if they so did.

   a. AD-IA Model
   b. ACCRA Cost of Living Index
   c. Invisible hand
   d. ACEA agreement

6. _____ was a Scottish moral philosopher and a pioneer of political economy. One of the key figures of the Scottish Enlightenment, Smith is the author of The Theory of Moral Sentiments and An Inquiry into the Nature and Causes of the Wealth of Nations. The latter, usually abbreviated as The Wealth of Nations, is considered his magnum opus and the first modern work of economics.

a. Alan Greenspan
b. Adolph Fischer
c. Adolf Hitler
d. Adam Smith

7. _____s is the social science that studies the production, distribution, and consumption of goods and services. The term _____s comes from the Ancient Greek οἰκονομία from οἶκος (oikos, 'house') + νόμος (nomos, 'custom' or 'law'), hence 'rules of the house(hold)'. Current _____ models developed out of the broader field of political economy in the late 19th century, owing to a desire to use an empirical approach more akin to the physical sciences.
   a. Energy economics
   b. Opportunity cost
   c. Economic
   d. Inflation

8. _____ is a branch of economics that uses microeconomic techniques to simultaneously determine allocative efficiency within an economy and the income distribution associated with it. It analyzes social welfare, however measured, in terms of economic activities of the individuals that comprise the theoretical society considered. As such, individuals, with associated economic activities, are the basic units for aggregating to social welfare, whether of a group, a community, or a society, and there is no 'social welfare' apart from the 'welfare' associated with its individual units.
   a. Tobit model
   b. Law of increasing costs
   c. General equilibrium
   d. Welfare economics

9. In economics, an _____ is a way of representing various distributions of resources. Edgeworth made his presentation in his famous book, Mathematical Psychics: An essay on the application of mathematics to the moral sciences, 1881. Edgeworth's original two axis depiction was developed into the now familiar box diagram by Pareto in 1906 and was popularized in a later exposition by Bowley.
   a. International Social Security Association
   b. Equivalent variation
   c. ACCRA Cost of Living Index
   d. Edgeworth box

10. _____ is a common concept in economics, and gives rise to derived concepts such as consumer debt. Generally _____ is defined by opposition to production. But the precise definition can vary because different schools of economists define production quite differently.
    a. Foreclosure data providers
    b. Consumption
    c. Federal Reserve Bank Notes
    d. Cash or share options

11. In economics, _____ is the transfer of income, wealth or property from some individuals to others.

One premise of _____ is that money should be distributed to benefit the poorer members of society, and that the rich have an obligation to assist the poor, thus creating a more financially egalitarian society. Another argument is that the rich exploit the poor or otherwise gain unfair benefits.

   a. Redistribution
   b. 100-year flood
   c. 1921 recession
   d. 130-30 fund

12. In microeconomics, _____ is quite simply the conversion of inputs into outputs. It is an economic process that uses resources to create a good or service that is suitable for exchange. This can include manufacturing, storing, shipping, and packaging.
    a. Production
    b. Solved
    c. MET
    d. Red Guards

Chapter 16. Equilibrium and Its Basic Welfare Properties

13. A _____ is the set of all possible input bundles that a firm can produce given its resources. Used as part of profit maximization calculations.
   a. Production set
   b. 100-year flood
   c. 1921 recession
   d. 130-30 fund

14. A _____ includes all possible consumption bundles that someone can afford given the prices of goods and the person's income level. The _____ is bounded above by the budget line.
   a. Budget set
   b. 130-30 fund
   c. Budget surplus
   d. 100-year flood

15. Economics:

   - _____,the desire to own something and the ability to pay for it
   - _____ curve,a graphic representation of a _____ schedule
   - _____ deposit, the money in checking accounts
   - _____ pull theory,the theory that inflation occurs when _____ for goods and services exceeds existing supplies
   - _____ schedule,a table that lists the quantity of a good a person will buy it each different price
   - _____ side economics,the school of economics at believes government spending and tax cuts open economy by raising _____

   a. McKesson ' Robbins scandal
   b. Production
   c. Variability
   d. Demand

16. In economics, _____ is a measure of the relative satisfaction from consumption of various goods and services. Given this measure, one may speak meaningfully of increasing or decreasing _____, and thereby explain economic behavior in terms of attempts to increase one's _____. For illustrative purposes, changes in _____ are sometimes expressed in units called utils.
   a. Utility function
   b. Ordinal utility
   c. Utility
   d. Expected utility hypothesis

17. While preferences are the conventional foundation of microeconomics, it is often convenient to represent preferences with a _____ and reason indirectly about preferences with _____s. Let X be the consumption set, the set of all mutually-exclusive packages the consumer could conceivably consume (such as an indifference curve map without the indifference curves.) The consumer's _____ $u : X \to \mathbf{R}$ ranks each package in the consumption set.
   a. Utility function
   b. Utility
   c. Ordinal utility
   d. Expected utility hypothesis

18. In economics, a consumer's preferences are said to be _____ if adding more of a good to the consumer's consumption bundle does not make him/her worse off. They are said to be strongly monotone if adding more of a good to the consumer's consumption bundle makes him/her strictly better off.

Note that in cases where the good in question is a 'bad' (i.e.undersirable) it is a simple matter to redefine the notion of the good as its negative.

Chapter 16. Equilibrium and Its Basic Welfare Properties

a. Compound Interest Treasury Notes
c. Basis of futures
b. Weakly monotone
d. Bank rescue package

19. In finance, _____ is a measure of the sensitivity of the duration of a bond to changes in interest rates. There is an inverse relationship between _____ and sensitivity - in general, the higher the _____ less sensitive the bond price is to interest rate shifts, the lower the _____, the more sensitive it is.

Duration is a linear measure or 1st derivative of how the price of a bond changes in response to interest rate changes.

a. Technocracy
c. Convexity
b. Rule
d. Russian financial crisis

20. A _____ provision refers to any program which seeks to provide a minimum level of income, service or other support for many marginalized groups such as the poor, elderly, and disabled people. _____ programs are undertaken by governments as well as non-governmental organizations (NGOs.) _____ payments and services are typically provided at the expense of taxpayers generally, funded by benefactors, or by compulsory enrollment of the poor themselves.

a. 1921 recession
c. 130-30 fund
b. 100-year flood
d. Social welfare

21. In economics, a _____ is a real-valued function that ranks conceivable social states (alternative complete descriptions of the society) from lowest to highest. Inputs of the function include any variables considered to affect welfare of the society (Sen, 1970, p. 33.)

a. Contract curve
c. Social welfare function
b. Frisch elasticity of labor supply
d. Gini coefficient

22. Loosely, the _____ is the change in the objective value of the optimal solution of an optimization problem obtained by relaxing the constraint by one unit. In a business application, a _____ is the maximum price that management is willing to pay for an extra unit of a given limited resource. For example, if a production line is already operating at its maximum 40 hour limit, the _____ would be the price of keeping the line operational for an additional hour.

a. Shadow price
c. 1921 recession
b. 100-year flood
d. 130-30 fund

23. _____ is the a method of technical and economic research of the systems for purpose to optimize a parity between system's consumer functions or properties and expenses to achieve those functions or properties.

This methodology for continuous perfection of production, industrial technologies, organizational structures was developed by Juryj Sobolev in 1948 at the 'Perm telephone factory'

- 1948 Juryj Sobolev - the first success in application of a method analysis at the 'Perm telephone factory' .
- 1949 - the first application for the invention as result of use of the new method.

Chapter 16. Equilibrium and Its Basic Welfare Properties

Today in economically developed countries practically each enterprise or the company use methodology of the kind of functional-cost analysis as a practice of the quality management, most full satisfying to principles of standards of series ISO 9000.

- Interest of consumer not in products itself, but the advantage which it will receive from its usage.
- The consumer aspires to reduce his expenses
- Functions needed by consumer can be executed in the various ways, and, hence, with various efficiency and expenses. Among possible alternatives of realization of functions exist such in which the parity of quality and the price is the optimal for the consumer.

The goal of _____ is achievement of the highest consumer satisfaction of production at simultaneous decrease in all kinds of industrial expenses Classical _____ has three English synonyms - Value Engineering, Value Management, Value Analysis.

a. Willingness to pay
c. Staple financing
b. Monopoly wage
d. Function cost analysis

24. In economics, the _____ is the rate at which a consumer is ready to give up one good in exchange for another good while maintaining the same level of satisfaction.

Under the standard assumption of neoclassical economics that goods and services are continuously divisible, the marginal rates of substitution will be the same regardless of the direction of exchange, and will correspond to the slope of an indifference curve (more precisely, to the slope multiplied by -1) passing through the consumption bundle in question, at that point: mathematically, it is the implicit derivative. MRS of Y for X is the amount of Y for which a consumer is willing to exchange for X locally.

a. Quality bias
c. Demand vacuum
b. Supply and demand
d. Marginal rate of substitution

25. _____ is a broad label that refers to any individuals or households that use goods and services generated within the economy. The concept of a _____ is used in different contexts, so that the usage and significance of the term may vary.

Typically when business people and economists talk of _____s they are talking about person as _____, an aggregated commodity item with little individuality other than that expressed in the buy/not-buy decision.

a. Consumer
c. 100-year flood
b. 1921 recession
d. 130-30 fund

26. A _____ is an object whose consumption increases the utility of the consumer, for which the quantity demanded exceeds the quantity supplied at zero price. _____s are usually modeled as having diminishing marginal utility. The first individual purchase has high utility; the second has less.

Chapter 16. Equilibrium and Its Basic Welfare Properties

a. Composite good
c. Merit good
b. Pie method
d. Good

27. In microeconomics, the _____ is the problem consumers face: 'how should I spend my money in order to maximize my utility?'

Suppose their consumption set, or the enumeration of all possible consumption bundles that could be selected if there are no budget constraints has L commodities and is limited to positive amounts of consumption of each

$$x \in \mathbf{R}_+^L .$$

Suppose also that the prices (p) of the L commodities are positive

$$p \in \mathbf{R}_+^L ,$$

and the consumer's wealth is w, then the set of all affordable packages, the budget set, is

$$B(p,w) = \{x \in \mathbf{R}_+^L : \langle p, x \rangle \leq w\} ,$$

where $\langle p, x \rangle$ is the inner product of p and x, or the total cost of consuming x of the products at price level p. The consumer would like to buy the best package of commodities it can afford. Suppose that the consumer's utility function (u) is a real valued function with domain of the commodity bundles, or

$$u : \mathbf{R}_+^L \to \mathbf{R} .$$

Then the consumer's optimal choices x(p, w) are the utility maximizing bundle that is in the budget set, or

$$x(p,w) = \operatorname{argmax}_{x^* \in B(p,w)} u(x^*)$$

a. Expenditure minimization problem
c. Utility maximization problem
b. Induced consumption
d. Income elasticity of demand

28. In economics and finance, _____ is the change in total cost that arises when the quantity produced changes by one unit. It is the cost of producing one more unit of a good. Mathematically, the _____ function is expressed as the first derivative of the total cost (TC) function with respect to quantity (Q.)

a. Khozraschyot
c. Variable cost
b. Marginal cost
d. Quality costs

29. _____ is one of the four Ps of the marketing mix. The other three aspects are product, promotion, and place. It is also a key variable in microeconomic price allocation theory.

Chapter 16. Equilibrium and Its Basic Welfare Properties

a. Point of total assumption
c. Pricing
b. Guaranteed Maximum Price
d. Premium pricing

30. A _____ is something for which there is demand, but which is supplied without qualitative differentiation across a market. It is a product that is the same no matter who produces it, such as petroleum, notebook paper, or milk. In other words, copper is copper.
    a. Commodity
    c. Soft commodity
    b. Hard commodity
    d. 100-year flood

31. _____ theory is a branch of theoretical economics. It seeks to explain the behavior of supply, demand and prices in a whole economy with several or many markets. It is often assumed that agents are price takers and in that setting two common notions of equilibrium exist: Walrasian (or competitive) equilibrium, and its generalization; a price equilibrium with transfers.
    a. New Keynesian economics
    c. Human capital
    b. Rational choice theory
    d. General equilibrium

32. _____ is a branch of theoretical economics. It seeks to explain the behavior of supply, demand and prices in a whole economy with several or many markets. It is often assumed that agents are price takers and in that setting two common notions of equilibrium exist: Walrasian (or competitive) equilibrium, and its generalization; a price equilibrium with transfers.
    a. General equilibrium theory
    c. Public economics
    b. Leading indicators
    d. Monetary economics

33. In economics, a _____ is a good that is non-rivaled and non-excludable. This means, respectively, that consumption of the good by one individual does not reduce availability of the good for consumption by others; and that no one can be effectively excluded from using the good. In the real world, there may be no such thing as an absolutely non-rivaled and non-excludable good; but economists think that some goods approximate the concept closely enough for the analysis to be economically useful.
    a. Happiness economics
    c. Public good
    b. Neoclassical synthesis
    d. Demand-pull theory

34. A _____ is defined in economics as a good that exhibits these properties:

    - Excludable - it is reasonably possible to prevent a class of consumers (e.g. those who have not paid for it) from consuming the good.
    - Rivalrous - consumptions by one consumer prevents simultaneous consumption by other consumers. _____s satisfies an individual want while public good satisfies a collective want of the society.

    A _____ is the opposite of a public good, as they are almost exclusively made for profit.

    An example of the _____ is bread: bread eaten by a given person cannot be consumed by another (rivalry), and it is easy for a baker to refuse to trade a loaf (excludable

    a. Positional goods
    c. Demerit good
    b. Pie method
    d. Private good

Chapter 16. Equilibrium and Its Basic Welfare Properties

35. In economics, a _____ occurs when, due to the economies of scale of a particular industry, the maximum efficiency of production and distribution is realized through a single supplier.

Natural monopolies arise where the largest supplier in an industry, often the first supplier in a market, has an overwhelming cost advantage over other actual or potential competitors. This tends to be the case in industries where capital costs predominate, creating economies of scale which are large in relation to the size of the market, and hence high barriers to entry; examples include water services and electricity.

- a. Common-pool resource
- b. Privatizing profits and socializing losses
- c. Natural monopoly
- d. Collective goods

36. In economics, a _____ exists when a specific individual or enterprise has sufficient control over a particular product or service to determine significantly the terms on which other individuals shall have access to it. Monopolies are thus characterized by a lack of economic competition for the good or service that they provide and a lack of viable substitute goods. The verb 'monopolize' refers to the process by which a firm gains persistently greater market share than what is expected under perfect competition.

- a. 130-30 fund
- b. Monopoly
- c. 1921 recession
- d. 100-year flood

37. In retail systems, the _____ represents the specific value that represents unit price purchased. This value is used as a key factor in determining profitability and in some stock market theories it is used in establishing the value of stock holding.

_____s appear in several forms, such as Actual Cost, Last Cost, Average Cost and Net realizable value.

- a. Facilitation payment
- b. Customer Demand Planning
- c. Ten bagger
- d. Cost price

Chapter 17. The Positive Theory of Equilibrium

1. In economics, an _____ is a way of representing various distributions of resources. Edgeworth made his presentation in his famous book, Mathematical Psychics: An essay on the application of mathematics to the moral sciences, 1881. Edgeworth's original two axis depiction was developed into the now familiar box diagram by Pareto in 1906 and was popularized in a later exposition by Bowley.
   a. International Social Security Association
   b. ACCRA Cost of Living Index
   c. Edgeworth box
   d. Equivalent variation

2. Economics:

   - _____, the desire to own something and the ability to pay for it
   - _____ curve, a graphic representation of a _____ schedule
   - _____ deposit, the money in checking accounts
   - _____ pull theory, the theory that inflation occurs when _____ for goods and services exceeds existing supplies
   - _____ schedule, a table that lists the quantity of a good a person will buy it each different price
   - _____ side economics, the school of economics at believes government spending and tax cuts open economy by raising _____

   a. McKesson ' Robbins scandal
   b. Production
   c. Demand
   d. Variability

3. In economics, _____ is when quantity demanded is more than quantity supplied. See Economic shortage.
   a. ACEA agreement
   b. AD-IA Model
   c. ACCRA Cost of Living Index
   d. Excess demand

4. _____ theory, pioneered by American economist Paul Samuelson, is a method by which it is possible to discern the best possible option on the basis of consumer behavior. Essentially, this means that the preferences of consumers can be revealed by their purchasing habits. _____ theory came about because the theories of consumer demand were based on a diminishing marginal rate of substitution (MRS.)
   a. Marginal rate of substitution
   b. Rational addiction
   c. Joint demand
   d. Revealed preference

5. _____ in economics and business is the result of an exchange and from that trade we assign a numerical monetary value to a good, service or asset. If Alice trades Bob 4 apples for an orange, the _____ of an orange is 4 apples. Inversely, the _____ of an apple is 1/4 oranges.
   a. Premium pricing
   b. Price war
   c. Price book
   d. Price

6. _____ is a broad label that refers to any individuals or households that use goods and services generated within the economy. The concept of a _____ is used in different contexts, so that the usage and significance of the term may vary.

Typically when business people and economists talk of _____s they are talking about person as _____, an aggregated commodity item with little individuality other than that expressed in the buy/not-buy decision.

Chapter 17. The Positive Theory of Equilibrium

a. 1921 recession
b. 100-year flood
c. 130-30 fund
d. Consumer

7. In microeconomics, _____ is quite simply the conversion of inputs into outputs. It is an economic process that uses resources to create a good or service that is suitable for exchange. This can include manufacturing, storing, shipping, and packaging.
a. MET
b. Production
c. Solved
d. Red Guards

8. A _____ is the set of all possible input bundles that a firm can produce given its resources. Used as part of profit maximization calculations.
a. 100-year flood
b. 1921 recession
c. 130-30 fund
d. Production set

9. _____s is the social science that studies the production, distribution, and consumption of goods and services. The term _____s comes from the Ancient Greek οá¼°κονομῖα from οá¼¶κος (oikos, 'house') + νÏŒμος (nomos, 'custom' or 'law'), hence 'rules of the house(hold)'. Current _____ models developed out of the broader field of political economy in the late 19th century, owing to a desire to use an empirical approach more akin to the physical sciences.
a. Economic
b. Energy economics
c. Inflation
d. Opportunity cost

10. _____ is a branch of economics that uses microeconomic techniques to simultaneously determine allocative efficiency within an economy and the income distribution associated with it. It analyzes social welfare, however measured, in terms of economic activities of the individuals that comprise the theoretical society considered. As such, individuals, with associated economic activities, are the basic units for aggregating to social welfare, whether of a group, a community, or a society, and there is no 'social welfare' apart from the 'welfare' associated with its individual units.
a. Welfare economics
b. General equilibrium
c. Tobit model
d. Law of increasing costs

11. Competitive market equilibrium is the traditional concept of economic equilibrium, appropriate for the analysis of commodity markets with flexible prices and many traders, and serving as the benchmark of efficiency in economic analysis. It relies crucially on the assumption of a competitive environment where each trader decides upon a quantity that is so small compared to the total quantity traded in the market that their individual transactions have no influence on the prices.Competitive markets are an ideal, a standard that other market structures are evaluated by.

A _____ consists of a vector of prices and an allocation such that given the prices, each trader by maximizing his objective function (profit, preferences) subject to his technological possibilities and resource constraints plans to trade into his part of the proposed allocation, and such that the prices make all net trades compatible with one another ('clear the market') by equating aggregate supply and demand for the commodities which are traded.

a. Product-Market Growth Matrix
b. Partial equilibrium
c. Market system
d. Competitive equilibrium

12. In neoclassical economics and microeconomics, _____ describes the perfect being a market in which there are many small firms, all producing homogeneous goods. In the short term, such markets are productively inefficient as output will not occur where mc is equal to ac, but allocatively efficient, as output under _____ will always occur where mc is equal to mr, and therefore where mc equals ar. However, in the long term, such markets are both allocatively and productively efficient.
   a. Law of supply
   b. Co-operative economics
   c. General equilibrium
   d. Perfect competition

13. In economics, the _____ functional form of production functions is widely used to represent the relationship of an output to inputs. It was proposed by Knut Wicksell (1851-1926), and tested against statistical evidence by Charles Cobb and Paul Douglas in 1900-1928.

For production, the function is

$$Y = AL^{\alpha}K^{\beta},$$

where:

- Y = total production (the monetary value of all goods produced in a year)
- L = labor input
- K = capital input
- A = total factor productivity
- α and β are the output elasticities of labor and capital, respectively. These values are constants determined by available technology.

Output elasticity measures the responsiveness of output to a change in levels of either labor or capital used in production, ceteris paribus. For example if α = 0.15, a 1% increase in labor would lead to approximately a 0.15% increase in output.

   a. Growth accounting
   b. Demand-pull theory
   c. Social savings
   d. Cobb-Douglas

14. The _____ is a result in General equilibrium economics. It states that the system of excess demand functions for an economy is not restricted by the usual rationality restrictions on individual demands in the economy. Thus microeconomic rationality assumptions have no equivalent macroeconomic implications.
   a. Regular economy
   b. Sonnenschein-Mantel-Debreu theorem
   c. Differential tax analysis
   d. Quantity adjustment

15. A _____ includes all possible consumption bundles that someone can afford given the prices of goods and the person's income level. The _____ is bounded above by the budget line.
   a. 130-30 fund
   b. Budget set
   c. Budget surplus
   d. 100-year flood

Chapter 17. The Positive Theory of Equilibrium

16. In finance, _____ is a measure of the sensitivity of the duration of a bond to changes in interest rates. There is an inverse relationship between _____ and sensitivity - in general, the higher the _____ less sensitive the bond price is to interest rate shifts, the lower the _____, the more sensitive it is.

Duration is a linear measure or 1st derivative of how the price of a bond changes in response to interest rate changes.

a. Rule
b. Russian financial crisis
c. Convexity
d. Technocracy

17. In economics, _____ is a measure of the relative satisfaction from consumption of various goods and services. Given this measure, one may speak meaningfully of increasing or decreasing _____, and thereby explain economic behavior in terms of attempts to increase one's _____. For illustrative purposes, changes in _____ are sometimes expressed in units called utils.

a. Ordinal utility
b. Utility function
c. Utility
d. Expected utility hypothesis

18. While preferences are the conventional foundation of microeconomics, it is often convenient to represent preferences with a _____ and reason indirectly about preferences with _____s. Let X be the consumption set, the set of all mutually-exclusive packages the consumer could conceivably consume (such as an indifference curve map without the indifference curves.) The consumer's _____ $u : X \to \mathbf{R}$ ranks each package in the consumption set.

a. Ordinal utility
b. Utility
c. Expected utility hypothesis
d. Utility function

19. _____ is an important concept in economics with broad applications in game theory, engineering and the social sciences. The term is named after Vilfredo Pareto, an Italian economist who used the concept in his studies of economic efficiency and income distribution. Informally, pareto efficient situations are those in which any change to make any person better off would make someone else worse off.

a. Lump of labour
b. Matching pennies
c. Perfect rationality
d. Pareto efficiency

20. In economics, _____ is the comparison of two different equilibrium states, before and after a change in some underlying exogenous parameter. As a study of statics it compares two different unchanging points, after they have changed. It does not study the motion towards equilibrium, nor the process of the change itself.

a. Social surplus
b. Comparative statics
c. Feasibility condition
d. Customer equity

21. In economics, _____ are a property of utility functions commonly represented in an indifference curve as a bulge toward the origin for normal goods. (A concave utility function appears to bulge away from the origin instead.) It roughly corresponds to the 'law' of diminishing marginal utility but uses modern theory to represent the concept.

a. Joint demand
b. Snob effect
c. Convex preferences
d. Deferred gratification

Chapter 17. The Positive Theory of Equilibrium

22. In game theory, _____ is a solution concept of a game involving two or more players, in which each player is assumed to know the equilibrium strategies of the other players, and no player has anything to gain by changing only his or her own strategy unilaterally. If each player has chosen a strategy and no player can benefit by changing his or her strategy while the other players keep theirs unchanged, then the current set of strategy choices and the corresponding payoffs constitute a _____.

Stated simply, Amy and Bill are in _____ if Amy is making the best decision she can, taking into account Bill's decision, and Bill is making the best decision he can, taking into account Amy's decision.

   a. Proper equilibrium
   b. Lump of labour
   c. Nash equilibrium
   d. Linear production game

23. _____ is a common concept in economics, and gives rise to derived concepts such as consumer debt. Generally _____ is defined by opposition to production. But the precise definition can vary because different schools of economists define production quite differently.
   a. Cash or share options
   b. Foreclosure data providers
   c. Federal Reserve Bank Notes
   d. Consumption

24. To _____ is to impose a financial charge or other levy upon a taxpayer by a state or the functional equivalent of a state.

_____es are also imposed by many subnational entities. _____es consist of direct _____ or indirect _____, and may be paid in money or as its labour equivalent (often but not always unpaid.)

   a. 100-year flood
   b. Tax
   c. 1921 recession
   d. 130-30 fund

25. To tax is to impose a financial charge or other levy upon a taxpayer by a state or the functional equivalent of a state.

_____ are also imposed by many subnational entities. _____ consist of direct tax or indirect tax, and may be paid in money or as its labour equivalent (often but not always unpaid.)

   a. 130-30 fund
   b. 100-year flood
   c. 1921 recession
   d. Taxes

26. In economics, _____ is the ratio of the percent change in one variable to the percent change in another variable. It is a tool for measuring the responsiveness of a function to changes in parameters in a relative way. Commonly analyzed are _____ of substitution, price and wealth.
   a. ACCRA Cost of Living Index
   b. Elasticity of demand
   c. ACEA agreement
   d. Elasticity

27. _____ is the elasticity of the ratio of two inputs to a production (or utility) function with respect to the ratio of their marginal products (or utilities.) It measures the curvature of an isoquant.
   a. Elasticity of substitution
   b. Indifference map
   c. Income elasticity of demand
   d. Indifference curve

Chapter 17. The Positive Theory of Equilibrium

28. A _____ is a type of economic equilibrium, where the clearance on the market of some specific goods is obtained independently from prices and quantities demanded and supplied in other markets. In other words, the prices of all substitutes and complements, as well as income levels of consumers are constant. Here the dynamic process is that prices adjust until supply equals demand.
　a. Partial equilibrium
　b. Horizontal market
　c. Market system
　d. Market depth

29. In economics, a _____ is a function that specifies the output of a firm, an industry, or an entire economy for all combinations of inputs. A meta-_____ compares the practice of the existing entities converting inputs X into output y to determine the most efficient practice _____ of the existing entities, whether the most efficient feasible practice production or the most efficient actual practice production. In either case, the maximum output of a technologically-determined production process is a mathematical function of input factors of production.
　a. Constant elasticity of substitution
　b. Short-run
　c. Post-Fordism
　d. Production function

Chapter 18. Some Foundations for Competitive Equilibria

1. Competitive market equilibrium is the traditional concept of economic equilibrium, appropriate for the analysis of commodity markets with flexible prices and many traders, and serving as the benchmark of efficiency in economic analysis. It relies crucially on the assumption of a competitive environment where each trader decides upon a quantity that is so small compared to the total quantity traded in the market that their individual transactions have no influence on the prices.Competitive markets are an ideal, a standard that other market structures are evaluated by.

A _____ consists of a vector of prices and an allocation such that given the prices, each trader by maximizing his objective function (profit, preferences) subject to his technological possibilities and resource constraints plans to trade into his part of the proposed allocation, and such that the prices make all net trades compatible with one another ('clear the market') by equating aggregate supply and demand for the commodities which are traded.

- a. Partial equilibrium
- b. Product-Market Growth Matrix
- c. Market system
- d. Competitive equilibrium

2. Given some endowment in an Edgeworth box, the _____ is the individually rational subset of the Pareto set. In other words, it is the set of Pareto efficient allocations in an economy. Also, any Walrasian equilibrium lies in the _____ of the Pareto set.
- a. Social welfare function
- b. Hidden Welfare State
- c. Missing market
- d. Contract curve

3. In economics, an _____ is a way of representing various distributions of resources. Edgeworth made his presentation in his famous book, Mathematical Psychics: An essay on the application of mathematics to the moral sciences, 1881. Edgeworth's original two axis depiction was developed into the now familiar box diagram by Pareto in 1906 and was popularized in a later exposition by Bowley.
- a. ACCRA Cost of Living Index
- b. International Social Security Association
- c. Edgeworth box
- d. Equivalent variation

4. _____s is the social science that studies the production, distribution, and consumption of goods and services. The term _____s comes from the Ancient Greek oá¼°κονομῖα from oá¼¶κος (oikos, 'house') + vĩŒμος (nomos, 'custom' or 'law'), hence 'rules of the house(hold)'. Current _____ models developed out of the broader field of political economy in the late 19th century, owing to a desire to use an empirical approach more akin to the physical sciences.
- a. Opportunity cost
- b. Inflation
- c. Energy economics
- d. Economic

5. _____ is a branch of economics that uses microeconomic techniques to simultaneously determine allocative efficiency within an economy and the income distribution associated with it. It analyzes social welfare, however measured, in terms of economic activities of the individuals that comprise the theoretical society considered. As such, individuals, with associated economic activities, are the basic units for aggregating to social welfare, whether of a group, a community, or a society, and there is no 'social welfare' apart from the 'welfare' associated with its individual units.
- a. Tobit model
- b. Welfare economics
- c. General equilibrium
- d. Law of increasing costs

6. _____ is an important concept in economics with broad applications in game theory, engineering and the social sciences. The term is named after Vilfredo Pareto, an Italian economist who used the concept in his studies of economic efficiency and income distribution. Informally, pareto efficient situations are those in which any change to make any person better off would make someone else worse off.

a. Matching pennies
c. Lump of labour
b. Perfect rationality
d. Pareto efficiency

7. _____ in economics and business is the result of an exchange and from that trade we assign a numerical monetary value to a good, service or asset. If Alice trades Bob 4 apples for an orange, the _____ of an orange is 4 apples. Inversely, the _____ of an apple is 1/4 oranges.

a. Price book
c. Price war
b. Premium pricing
d. Price

Chapter 18. Some Foundations for Competitive Equilibria 103

8. A _____ is:

- Rewrite _____, in generative grammar and computer science
- Standardization, a formal and widely-accepted statement, fact, definition, or qualification
- Operation, a determinate _____ for performing a mathematical operation and obtaining a certain result (Mathematics, Logic)
    - Unary operation
    - Binary operation
- _____ of inference, a function from sets of formulae to formulae (Mathematics, Logic)
- _____ of thumb, principle with broad application that is not intended to be strictly accurate or reliable for every situation. Also often simply referred to as a _____
- Moral, an atomic element of a moral code for guiding choices in human behavior
- Heuristic, a quantized '_____' which shows a tendency or probability for successful function
- A regulation, as in sports
- A Production _____, as in computer science
- Procedural law, a _____ set governing the application of laws to cases
    - A law, which may informally be called a '_____'
    - A court ruling, a decision by a court
- In the U.S. Government, a regulation mandated by Congress, but written or expanded upon by the Executive Branch.
- Norm (sociology), an informal but widely accepted _____, concept, truth, definition, or qualification (social norms, legal norms, coding norms)
- Norm (philosophy), a kind of sentence or a reason to act, feel or believe
- 'Rulership' is the concept of governance by a government:
    - Military _____, governance by a military body
    - Monastic _____, a collection of precepts that guides the life of monks or nuns in a religious order where the superior holds the place of Christ
- Slide _____

- '_____,' a song by Ayumi Hamasaki
- '_____,' a song by rapper Nas
- '_____s,' an album by the band The Whitest Boy Alive
- _____s: Pyaar Ka Superhit Formula, a 2003 Bollywood film
- ruler, an instrument for measuring lengths
- _____, a component of an astrolabe, circumferator or similar instrument
- The _____s, a bestselling self-help book
- _____ Project (Run Up-to-date Linux Everywhere), a project that aims to use up-to-date Linux software on old PCs
- _____ engine, a software system that helps managing business _____s
- Ja _____, a hip hop artist
    - R.U.L.E., a 2005 greatest hits album by rapper Ja _____
- '_____s,' a KMFDM song

a. Demand
c. Procter ' Gamble
b. Technocracy
d. Rule

Chapter 18. Some Foundations for Competitive Equilibria

9. _____ is an economic model used to describe an industry structure in which companies compete on the amount of output they will produce, which they decide on independently of each other and at the same time. It is named after Antoine Augustin Cournot (1801-1877) after he observed competition in a spring water duopoly. It has the following features:

- There is more than one firm and all firms produce a homogeneous product, i.e. there is no product differentiation;
- Firms do not cooperate, i.e. there is no collusion;
- Firms have market power, i.e. each firm's output decision affects the good's price;
- The number of firms is fixed;
- Firms compete in quantities, and choose quantities simultaneously;
- The firms are economically rational and act strategically, usually seeking to maximize profit given their competitors' decisions.

An essential assumption of this model is that each firm aims to maximize profits, based on the expectation that its own output decision will not have an effect on the decisions of its rivals. Price is a commonly known decreasing function of total output.

a. 1921 recession
b. 130-30 fund
c. 100-year flood
d. Cournot competition

10. _____ theory is a branch of theoretical economics. It seeks to explain the behavior of supply, demand and prices in a whole economy with several or many markets. It is often assumed that agents are price takers and in that setting two common notions of equilibrium exist: Walrasian (or competitive) equilibrium, and its generalization; a price equilibrium with transfers.

a. Rational choice theory
b. Human capital
c. General equilibrium
d. New Keynesian economics

11. A _____ includes all possible consumption bundles that someone can afford given the prices of goods and the person's income level. The _____ is bounded above by the budget line.

a. 100-year flood
b. 130-30 fund
c. Budget surplus
d. Budget set

12. Economics:

- _____, the desire to own something and the ability to pay for it
- _____ curve, a graphic representation of a _____ schedule
- _____ deposit, the money in checking accounts
- _____ pull theory, the theory that inflation occurs when _____ for goods and services exceeds existing supplies
- _____ schedule, a table that lists the quantity of a good a person will buy it each different price
- _____ side economics, the school of economics at believes government spending and tax cuts open economy by raising _____

a. McKesson ' Robbins scandal
b. Variability
c. Production
d. Demand

13. In microeconomics, _____ is quite simply the conversion of inputs into outputs. It is an economic process that uses resources to create a good or service that is suitable for exchange. This can include manufacturing, storing, shipping, and packaging.

   a. Solved
   b. Red Guards
   c. MET
   d. Production

14. In economics, _____ is the transfer of income, wealth or property from some individuals to others.

One premise of _____ is that money should be distributed to benefit the poorer members of society, and that the rich have an obligation to assist the poor, thus creating a more financially egalitarian society. Another argument is that the rich exploit the poor or otherwise gain unfair benefits.

   a. Redistribution
   b. 100-year flood
   c. 1921 recession
   d. 130-30 fund

15. _____ in economics refers to metrics and measures of output from production processes, per unit of input. Labor _____, for example, is typically measured as a ratio of output per labor-hour, an input. _____ may be conceived of as a metrics of the technical or engineering efficiency of production.

   a. Piece work
   b. Production-possibility frontier
   c. Fordism
   d. Productivity

16. In game theory, a _____, named in honour of Lloyd Shapley, who introduced it in 1953, describes one approach to the fair allocation of gains obtained by cooperation among several actors.

The setup is as follows: a coalition of actors cooperates, and obtains a certain overall gain from that cooperation. Since some actors may contribute more to the coalition than others, the question arises how to distribute fairly the gains among the actors.

   a. Smart market
   b. Fictitious play
   c. Markov perfect
   d. Shapley value

17. _____ is the a method of technical and economic research of the systems for purpose to optimize a parity between system's consumer functions or properties and expenses to achieve those functions or properties.

This methodology for continuous perfection of production, industrial technologies, organizational structures was developed by Juryj Sobolev in 1948 at the 'Perm telephone factory'

- 1948 Juryj Sobolev - the first success in application of a method analysis at the 'Perm telephone factory' .
- 1949 - the first application for the invention as result of use of the new method.

Chapter 18. Some Foundations for Competitive Equilibria

Today in economically developed countries practically each enterprise or the company use methodology of the kind of functional-cost analysis as a practice of the quality management, most full satisfying to principles of standards of series ISO 9000.

- Interest of consumer not in products itself, but the advantage which it will receive from its usage.
- The consumer aspires to reduce his expenses
- Functions needed by consumer can be executed in the various ways, and, hence, with various efficiency and expenses. Among possible alternatives of realization of functions exist such in which the parity of quality and the price is the optimal for the consumer.

The goal of _____ is achievement of the highest consumer satisfaction of production at simultaneous decrease in all kinds of industrial expenses Classical _____ has three English synonyms - Value Engineering, Value Management, Value Analysis.

a. Function cost analysis
c. Willingness to pay
b. Staple financing
d. Monopoly wage

18. In economics, _____ is a measure of the relative satisfaction from consumption of various goods and services. Given this measure, one may speak meaningfully of increasing or decreasing _____, and thereby explain economic behavior in terms of attempts to increase one's _____. For illustrative purposes, changes in _____ are sometimes expressed in units called utils.

a. Utility function
c. Utility
b. Ordinal utility
d. Expected utility hypothesis

19. _____ has several particular meanings:

- in mathematics
    - _____ function
    - Euler _____
    - _____
    - _____ subgroup
    - method of _____s (partial differential equations)
- in physics and engineering
    - any _____ curve that shows the relationship between certain input- and output parameters, e.g.
    - an I-V or current-voltage _____ is the current in a circuit as a function of the applied voltage
    - Receiver-Operator _____
- in fiction
    - in Dungeons ' Dragons, _____ is another name for ability score

a. Russian financial crisis
c. Technocracy
b. Characteristic
d. Demand

Chapter 18. Some Foundations for Competitive Equilibria

20. The _____ is the apparent contradiction that although water is on the whole more useful, in terms of survival, than diamonds, diamonds command a higher price in the market. The economist Adam Smith is often considered to be the classic presenter of this paradox. Nicolaus Copernicus, John Locke, John Law and others had previously tried to explain the disparity.
   a. Paradox of value
   b. 100-year flood
   c. 130-30 fund
   d. St. Petersburg paradox

21. _____ is a branch of applied mathematics that is used in the social sciences (most notably economics), biology, engineering, political science, international relations, computer science, and philosophy. _____ attempts to mathematically capture behavior in strategic situations, in which an individual's success in making choices depends on the choices of others. While initially developed to analyze competitions in which one individual does better at another's expense (zero sum games), it has been expanded to treat a wide class of interactions, which are classified according to several criteria.
   a. Game theory
   b. Discriminatory price auction
   c. Dollar auction
   d. Proper equilibrium

22. In calculus, a function f defined on a subset of the real numbers with real values is called _____, if for all x and y such that x >≤ y one has f(x) >≤ f(y), so f preserves the order. In layman's terms, the sign of the slope is always positive (the curve tending upwards) or zero (i.e., non-decreasing, or asymptotic, or depicted as a horizontal, flat line) Likewise, a function is called monotonically decreasing (non-increasing) if, whenever x >≤ y, then f(x) >≥ f(y), so it reverses the order.
   a. 1921 recession
   b. 130-30 fund
   c. 100-year flood
   d. Monotonic

23. In economics, a _____ is a function that specifies the output of a firm, an industry, or an entire economy for all combinations of inputs. A meta-_____ compares the practice of the existing entities converting inputs X into output y to determine the most efficient practice _____ of the existing entities, whether the most efficient feasible practice production or the most efficient actual practice production. In either case, the maximum output of a technologically-determined production process is a mathematical function of input factors of production.
   a. Short-run
   b. Post-Fordism
   c. Constant elasticity of substitution
   d. Production function

24. _____ or Equalism is a political doctrine that holds that all people should be treated as equals and have the same political, economic, social, and civil rights. Generally it applies to being held equal under the law and society at large. In actual practice, one may be considered an egalitarian in most areas listed below, even if not subscribing to equality in every possible area of individual difference.
   a. ACCRA Cost of Living Index
   b. Egalitarianism
   c. ACEA agreement
   d. AD-IA Model

25. _____ is the term denoting either an entrance or changes which are inserted into a system and which activate/modify a process. It is an abstract concept, used in the modeling, system(s) design and system(s) exploitation. It is usually connected with other terms, e.g., _____ field, _____ variable, _____ parameter, _____ value, _____ signal, _____ device and _____ file.
   a. ACEA agreement
   b. ACCRA Cost of Living Index
   c. AD-IA Model
   d. Input

Chapter 19. General Equilibrium Under Uncertainty

1. _____ theory is a branch of theoretical economics. It seeks to explain the behavior of supply, demand and prices in a whole economy with several or many markets. It is often assumed that agents are price takers and in that setting two common notions of equilibrium exist: Walrasian (or competitive) equilibrium, and its generalization; a price equilibrium with transfers.
   a. New Keynesian economics
   b. Rational choice theory
   c. General equilibrium
   d. Human capital

2. _____ is a concept with somewhat disparate meanings in several fields. It also has a common meaning which has a loose connection with some of those more definite meanings.

   Casually, it is typically used to denote a lack of order, or purpose, or cause.

   a. 1921 recession
   b. 100-year flood
   c. 130-30 fund
   d. Randomness

3. In mathematics, _____ are used in the study of chance and probability. They were developed to assist in the analysis of games of chance, stochastic events, and the results of scientific experiments by capturing only the mathematical properties necessary to answer probabilistic questions. Further formalizations have firmly grounded the entity in the theoretical domains of mathematics by making use of measure theory.
   a. 100-year flood
   b. 130-30 fund
   c. 1921 recession
   d. Random variables

4. Economics:

   - _____, the desire to own something and the ability to pay for it
   - _____ curve, a graphic representation of a _____ schedule
   - _____ deposit, the money in checking accounts
   - _____ pull theory, the theory that inflation occurs when _____ for goods and services exceeds existing supplies
   - _____ schedule, a table that lists the quantity of a good a person will buy it each different price
   - _____ side economics, the school of economics at believes government spending and tax cuts open economy by raising _____

   a. Production
   b. Demand
   c. McKesson ' Robbins scandal
   d. Variability

5. A _____ is an economy based on the division of labor in which the prices of goods and services are determined in a free price system set by supply and demand. This is often contrasted with a planned economy, in which a central government determines the price of goods and services using a fixed price system. Market economies are contrasted with mixed economy where the price system is not entirely free but under some government control that is not extensive enough to constitute a planned economy.
   a. Commons-based peer production
   b. Network Economy
   c. Nutritional Economics
   d. Market economy

Chapter 19. General Equilibrium Under Uncertainty

6. In game theory, _____ is a solution concept of a game involving two or more players, in which each player is assumed to know the equilibrium strategies of the other players, and no player has anything to gain by changing only his or her own strategy unilaterally. If each player has chosen a strategy and no player can benefit by changing his or her strategy while the other players keep theirs unchanged, then the current set of strategy choices and the corresponding payoffs constitute a _____.

Stated simply, Amy and Bill are in _____ if Amy is making the best decision she can, taking into account Bill's decision, and Bill is making the best decision he can, taking into account Amy's decision.

   a. Nash equilibrium
   b. Lump of labour
   c. Linear production game
   d. Proper equilibrium

7. A _____ is something for which there is demand, but which is supplied without qualitative differentiation across a market. It is a product that is the same no matter who produces it, such as petroleum, notebook paper, or milk. In other words, copper is copper.
   a. Soft commodity
   b. 100-year flood
   c. Hard commodity
   d. Commodity

8. In microeconomics, _____ is quite simply the conversion of inputs into outputs. It is an economic process that uses resources to create a good or service that is suitable for exchange. This can include manufacturing, storing, shipping, and packaging.
   a. Red Guards
   b. MET
   c. Solved
   d. Production

9. In economics, _____ is a measure of the relative satisfaction from consumption of various goods and services. Given this measure, one may speak meaningfully of increasing or decreasing _____, and thereby explain economic behavior in terms of attempts to increase one's _____. For illustrative purposes, changes in _____ are sometimes expressed in units called utils.
   a. Utility
   b. Utility function
   c. Ordinal utility
   d. Expected utility hypothesis

10. While preferences are the conventional foundation of microeconomics, it is often convenient to represent preferences with a _____ and reason indirectly about preferences with _____s. Let X be the consumption set, the set of all mutually-exclusive packages the consumer could conceivably consume (such as an indifference curve map without the indifference curves.) The consumer's _____ $u : X \to \mathbf{R}$ ranks each package in the consumption set.
   a. Ordinal utility
   b. Expected utility hypothesis
   c. Utility
   d. Utility function

11. In statistics, the _____ problem occurs when one considers a set of statistical inferences simultaneously. Errors in inference, including confidence intervals that fail to include their corresponding population parameters are more likely to occur when one considers the family as a whole. Several statistical techniques have been developed to prevent this from happening, allowing significance levels for single and _____ to be directly compared.
   a. False discovery rate
   b. Multiple comparisons
   c. Hypotheses suggested by the data
   d. Familywise error rate

12. In economics, an _____ is a way of representing various distributions of resources. Edgeworth made his presentation in his famous book, Mathematical Psychics: An essay on the application of mathematics to the moral sciences, 1881. Edgeworth's original two axis depiction was developed into the now familiar box diagram by Pareto in 1906 and was popularized in a later exposition by Bowley.
   a. Equivalent variation
   b. International Social Security Association
   c. Edgeworth box
   d. ACCRA Cost of Living Index

13. _____ is an important concept in economics with broad applications in game theory, engineering and the social sciences. The term is named after Vilfredo Pareto, an Italian economist who used the concept in his studies of economic efficiency and income distribution. Informally, pareto efficient situations are those in which any change to make any person better off would make someone else worse off.
   a. Perfect rationality
   b. Matching pennies
   c. Lump of labour
   d. Pareto efficiency

14. The _____ is the over-the-counter financial market in contracts for future delivery, so called forward contracts. Forward contracts are personalized between parties. The _____ is a general term used to describe the informal market by which these contracts are entered into.
   a. Forward market
   b. Market data
   c. Delta neutral
   d. Convertible arbitrage

15. The _____ or cash market is a commodities or securities market in which goods are sold for cash and delivered immediately. Contracts bought and sold on these markets are immediately effective. _____ s can operate wherever the infrastructure exists to conduct the transaction.
   a. Foreign exchange trading
   b. Currency band
   c. Triangular arbitrage
   d. Spot market

16. A _____ includes all possible consumption bundles that someone can afford given the prices of goods and the person's income level. The _____ is bounded above by the budget line.
   a. 130-30 fund
   b. Budget surplus
   c. 100-year flood
   d. Budget set

17. _____ is an economic concept defined by economist Roy Radner in the context of general equilibrium. The concept is an extension of the Arrow-Debreu equilibrium and the base for the first consistent incomplete markets framework.

The departure from the Arrow-Debreu framework are two-fold: (1) uncertainty is explicitly modelled through a tree structure (or equivalent filtration) rending passage of time and resolution of uncertainty explicit, (2) budget feasibility is no longer defined as affordability but through explicit trading of financial instruments.

   a. Flight-to-liquidity
   b. January effect
   c. Cass criterion
   d. Radner equilibrium

18. _____ is an assumption used in many contemporary macroeconomic models, and also in other areas of contemporary economics and game theory and in other applications of rational choice theory.

Chapter 19. General Equilibrium Under Uncertainty

Since most macroeconomic models today study decisions over many periods, the expectations of workers, consumers, and firms about future economic conditions are an essential part of the model. How to model these expectations has long been controversial, and it is well known that the macroeconomic predictions of the model may differ depending on the assumptions made about expectations

    a. Minimum wage   b. Balanced-growth equilibrium
    c. Potential output   d. Rational Expectations

19. In business and accounting, _____ are everything of value that is owned by a person or company. It is a claim on the property your income of a borrower. The balance sheet of a firm records the monetary value of the _____ owned by the firm.
    a. ACEA agreement   b. Amortization schedule
    c. Assets   d. ACCRA Cost of Living Index

20. _____s are financial contracts whose values are derived from the value of something else (known as the underlying.) The underlying value on which a _____ is based can be an asset (e.g., commodities, equities (stocks), residential mortgages, commercial real estate, loans, bonds), an index (e.g., interest rates, exchange rates, stock market indices, consumer price index (CPI) -- see inflation _____s), weather conditions bonds or other forms of credit.
    a. Derivative   b. Second derivative
    c. 130-30 fund   d. 100-year flood

21. A _____ is a financial contract between two parties, the buyer and the seller of this type of option. It is the option to buy shares of stock at a specified time in the future.Often it is simply labeled a 'call'. The buyer of the option has the right, but not the obligation to buy an agreed quantity of a particular commodity or financial instrument (the underlying instrument) from the seller of the option at a certain time (the expiration date) for a certain price (the strike price.)
    a. Put option   b. Moneyness
    c. Synthetic underlying position   d. Call option

22. In options, the _____ is a key variable in a derivatives contract between two parties. Where the contract requires delivery of the underlying instrument, the trade will be at the _____, regardless of the spot price (market price) of the underlying instrument at that time.

Definition - The fixed price at which the owner of an option can purchase, in the case of a call in the case of a put, the underlying security or commodity.

    a. Calendar spread   b. Binary option
    c. Married put   d. Strike price

23. _____ in economics and business is the result of an exchange and from that trade we assign a numerical monetary value to a good, service or asset. If Alice trades Bob 4 apples for an orange, the _____ of an orange is 4 apples. Inversely, the _____ of an apple is 1/4 oranges.
    a. Price book   b. Price war
    c. Premium pricing   d. Price

Chapter 19. General Equilibrium Under Uncertainty

24. A security is a fungible, negotiable instrument representing financial value. _____ are broadly categorized into debt _____; equity _____, e.g., common stocks; and derivative (finance) contracts such as forwards, futures, options and swaps. The company or other entity issuing the security is called the issuer.

   a. Settlement risk
   b. Securities
   c. Pass-Through Certificates
   d. Red herring prospectus

25. A _____ represents the combinations of goods and services that a consumer can purchase given current prices and his income. Consumer theory uses the concepts of a _____ and a preference map to analyze consumer choices. Both concepts have a ready graphical representation in the two-good case.

   a. Revealed preference
   b. Joint demand
   c. Quality bias
   d. Budget constraint

26. In economics, game theory, and decision theory the _____ theorem or _____ hypothesis predicts that the 'betting preferences' of people with regard to uncertain outcomes (gambles) can be described by a mathematical relation which takes into account the size of a payout (whether in money or other goods), the probability of occurrence, risk aversion, and the different utility of the same payout to people with different assets or personal preferences. It is a more sophisticated theory than simply predicting that choices will be made based on expected value (which takes into account only the size of the payout and the probability of occurrence.)

Daniel Bernoulli described the complete theory in 1738.

   a. Expected utility hypothesis
   b. Ordinal utility
   c. Expected utility
   d. Utility

27. In mathematical optimization, the method of _____s provides a strategy for finding the maximum/minimum of a function subject to constraints.

For example, consider the optimization problem

$$\text{maximize } f(x, y)$$
$$\text{subject to } g(x, y) = c.$$

We introduce a new variable (λ) called a _____, and study the Lagrange function defined by

$$\Lambda(x, y, \lambda) = f(x, y) + \lambda\Big(g(x, y) - c\Big).$$

(λ may be either added or subtracted.) If (x,y)′ is a maximum for the original constrained problem, then there exists a λ such that (x,y,λ)′ is a stationary point for the Lagrange function (stationary points are those points where the partial derivatives of Λ are zero.)

   a. Lagrange multiplier
   b. Radfar ratio
   c. 130-30 fund
   d. 100-year flood

Chapter 19. General Equilibrium Under Uncertainty

28. In economics, a consumer's preferences are said to be _____ if adding more of a good to the consumer's consumption bundle does not make him/her worse off. They are said to be strongly monotone if adding more of a good to the consumer's consumption bundle makes him/her strictly better off.

Note that in cases where the good in question is a 'bad' (i.e.undersirable) it is a simple matter to redefine the notion of the good as its negative.

a. Basis of futures
b. Weakly monotone
c. Bank rescue package
d. Compound Interest Treasury Notes

29. In economics and finance, _____ is the practice of taking advantage of a price differential between two or more markets: striking a combination of matching deals that capitalize upon the imbalance, the profit being the difference between the market prices. When used by academics, an _____ is a transaction that involves no negative cash flow at any probabilistic or temporal state and a positive cash flow in at least one state; in simple terms, a risk-free profit. A person who engages in _____ is called an arbitrageur--such as a bank or brokerage firm.

a. Arbitrage
b. Alternext
c. Options Price Reporting Authority
d. Electronic trading

30. _____ is one of the four Ps of the marketing mix. The other three aspects are product, promotion, and place. It is also a key variable in microeconomic price allocation theory.

a. Guaranteed Maximum Price
b. Pricing
c. Point of total assumption
d. Premium pricing

31. The Theory of _____ is an extension of the general equilibrium approach to intertemporal economies with uncertainty, where the set of available contracts which can be used to transfer wealth across time is limited relative to the possible probabilistic states that an economy might find itself in. Unlike in the standard Arrow-Debreu model where all trade is planned at beginning of time. These agents can do this for their descendents at the beginning of time in the Classical model (i.e. with complete markets) because agents are assumed to have costless contractual enforcement and perfect calculations along with perfect knowledge of the likelihood of all possible future states (across an unlimited range of contracts.)

a. Income distribution
b. Equity trading
c. Investment goods
d. Incomplete markets

32. _____ is the strategy an investor uses to distribute his or her investments among various classes of investment vehicles (e.g., stocks and bonds.)

A large part of financial planning is finding an _____ that is appropriate for a given person in terms of their appetite for and ability to shoulder risk. This can depend on various factors; see investor profile.

a. Investor awareness
b. Equity repositioning
c. Asset allocation
d. Investing online

33. In microeconomics, the _____ is the problem consumers face: 'how should I spend my money in order to maximize my utility?'

Chapter 19. General Equilibrium Under Uncertainty

Suppose their consumption set, or the enumeration of all possible consumption bundles that could be selected if there are no budget constraints has L commodities and is limited to positive amounts of consumption of each

$$x \in \mathbf{R}_+^L .$$

Suppose also that the prices (p) of the L commodities are positive

$$p \in \mathbf{R}_+^L ,$$

and the consumer's wealth is w, then the set of all affordable packages, the budget set, is

$$B(p,w) = \{x \in \mathbf{R}_+^L : \langle p, x \rangle \leq w\} ,$$

where $\langle p, x \rangle$ is the inner product of p and x, or the total cost of consuming x of the products at price level p. The consumer would like to buy the best package of commodities it can afford. Suppose that the consumer's utility function (u) is a real valued function with domain of the commodity bundles, or

$$u : \mathbf{R}_+^L \to \mathbf{R} .$$

Then the consumer's optimal choices x(p, w) are the utility maximizing bundle that is in the budget set, or

$$x(p,w) = \mathrm{argmax}_{x^* \in B(p,w)} u(x^*) .$$

a. Income elasticity of demand
c. Induced consumption
b. Expenditure minimization problem
d. Utility maximization problem

34. _____ is the price at which an asset would trade in a competitive Walrasian auction setting. _____ is often used interchangeably with open _____, fair value or fair _____, although these terms have distinct definitions in different standards, and may differ in some circumstances.

International Valuation Standards defines _____ as 'the estimated amount for which a property should exchange on the date of valuation between a willing buyer and a willing seller in an arm's-length transaction after proper marketing wherein the parties had each acted knowledgeably, prudently, and without compulsion.'

_____ is a concept distinct from market price, which is 'the price at which one can transact', while _____ is 'the true underlying value' according to theoretical standards.

a. Secured loan
c. Netting
b. Market value
d. Personal financial management

Chapter 19. General Equilibrium Under Uncertainty

35. _____ is the a method of technical and economic research of the systems for purpose to optimize a parity between system's consumer functions or properties and expenses to achieve those functions or properties.

This methodology for continuous perfection of production, industrial technologies, organizational structures was developed by Juryj Sobolev in 1948 at the 'Perm telephone factory'

- 1948 Juryj Sobolev - the first success in application of a method analysis at the 'Perm telephone factory' .
- 1949 - the first application for the invention as result of use of the new method.

Today in economically developed countries practically each enterprise or the company use methodology of the kind of functional-cost analysis as a practice of the quality management, most full satisfying to principles of standards of series ISO 9000.

- Interest of consumer not in products itself, but the advantage which it will receive from its usage.
- The consumer aspires to reduce his expenses
- Functions needed by consumer can be executed in the various ways, and, hence, with various efficiency and expenses. Among possible alternatives of realization of functions exist such in which the parity of quality and the price is the optimal for the consumer.

The goal of _____ is achievement of the highest consumer satisfaction of production at simultaneous decrease in all kinds of industrial expenses Classical _____ has three English synonyms - Value Engineering, Value Management, Value Analysis.

a. Staple financing
b. Willingness to pay
c. Monopoly wage
d. Function cost analysis

36. The _____ or spot rate of a commodity, a security or a currency is the price that is quoted for immediate (spot) settlement (payment and delivery.) Spot settlement is normally one or two business days from trade date. This is in contrast with the forward price established in a forward contract or futures contract, where contract terms (price) are set now, but delivery and payment will occur at a future date.

a. Minimum acceptable rate of return
b. Market saturation
c. Paper trading
d. Spot price

Chapter 20. Equilibrium and Time

1. _____ is a common concept in economics, and gives rise to derived concepts such as consumer debt. Generally _____ is defined by opposition to production. But the precise definition can vary because different schools of economists define production quite differently.
   a. Consumption
   b. Foreclosure data providers
   c. Cash or share options
   d. Federal Reserve Bank Notes

2. Discounting is a financial mechanism in which a debtor obtains the right to delay payments to a creditor, for a defined period of time, in exchange for a charge or fee. Essentially, the party that owes money in the present purchases the right to delay the payment until some future date. The _____, or charge, is simply the difference between the original amount owed in the present and the amount that has to be paid in the future to settle the debt.
   a. Certified Risk Manager
   b. Reinsurance
   c. Discount
   d. Reliability theory

3. In economics, _____ is a measure of the relative satisfaction from consumption of various goods and services. Given this measure, one may speak meaningfully of increasing or decreasing _____, and thereby explain economic behavior in terms of attempts to increase one's _____. For illustrative purposes, changes in _____ are sometimes expressed in units called utils.
   a. Utility function
   b. Expected utility hypothesis
   c. Ordinal utility
   d. Utility

4. The _____ is 'the basic residential unit in which economic production, consumption, inheritance, child rearing, and shelter are organized and carried out'; [the _____] 'may or may not be synonomous with family'.

   The _____ is the basic unit of analysis in many social, microeconomic and government models. The term refers to all individuals who live in the same dwelling.

   a. 130-30 fund
   b. Household
   c. Family economics
   d. 100-year flood

5. In microeconomics, _____ is quite simply the conversion of inputs into outputs. It is an economic process that uses resources to create a good or service that is suitable for exchange. This can include manufacturing, storing, shipping, and packaging.
   a. Red Guards
   b. Solved
   c. MET
   d. Production

6. A _____ is an intellectual property right to protect inventions. This right is available in a number of national legislations, such as Argentina, Austria, Brazil, Chile, China, Denmark, Finland, France, Germany, Hungary, Italy, Japan, Malaysia, Mexico, Morocco, Philippines, Poland, Portugal, Russia, South Korea, Spain, Taiwan, Uzbekistan, etc. It is very similar to the patent, but usually has a shorter term and less stringent patentability requirements.
   a. United Kingdom labour law
   b. Employment discrimination law in the United Kingdom
   c. Assigned risk
   d. Utility model

7. _____ is the deliberate pursuit of the interests or welfare of others or the public interest.

The concept has a long history in philosophical and ethical thought, and has more recently become a topic for psychologists, sociologists, evolutionary biologists, and ethologists. While ideas about _____ from one field can have an impact on the other fields, the different methods and focuses of these fields lead to different perspectives on _____.

a. AD-IA Model
b. ACEA agreement
c. ACCRA Cost of Living Index
d. Altruism

8. A _____ is the set of all possible input bundles that a firm can produce given its resources. Used as part of profit maximization calculations.
a. 1921 recession
b. 130-30 fund
c. 100-year flood
d. Production set

9. While preferences are the conventional foundation of microeconomics, it is often convenient to represent preferences with a _____ and reason indirectly about preferences with _____s. Let X be the consumption set, the set of all mutually-exclusive packages the consumer could conceivably consume (such as an indifference curve map without the indifference curves.) The consumer's _____ $u : X \rightarrow \mathbf{R}$ ranks each package in the consumption set.
a. Expected utility hypothesis
b. Utility
c. Ordinal utility
d. Utility function

10. _____ in economics and business is the result of an exchange and from that trade we assign a numerical monetary value to a good, service or asset. If Alice trades Bob 4 apples for an orange, the _____ of an orange is 4 apples. Inversely, the _____ of an apple is 1/4 oranges.
a. Price
b. Premium pricing
c. Price book
d. Price war

11. In economics, _____ is the process by which a firm determines the price and output level that returns the greatest profit. There are several approaches to this problem. The total revenue--total cost method relies on the fact that profit equals revenue minus cost, and the marginal revenue--marginal cost method is based on the fact that total profit in a perfectly competitive market reaches its maximum point where marginal revenue equals marginal cost.
a. 100-year flood
b. Profit margin
c. Normal profit
d. Profit maximization

12. _____s is the social science that studies the production, distribution, and consumption of goods and services. The term _____s comes from the Ancient Greek oá¼°κονομῖα from oá¼¶κος (oikos, 'house') + vÏŒμος (nomos, 'custom' or 'law'), hence 'rules of the house(hold)'. Current _____ models developed out of the broader field of political economy in the late 19th century, owing to a desire to use an empirical approach more akin to the physical sciences.
a. Economic
b. Inflation
c. Energy economics
d. Opportunity cost

13. In economics, the concept of the _____ refers to the decision-making time frame of a firm in which at least one factor of production is fixed. Costs which are fixed in the _____ have no impact on a firms decisions. For example a firm can raise output by increasing the amount of labour through overtime.

a. Hicks-neutral technical change
c. Productivity model
b. Product Pipeline
d. Short-run

14. _____ is a branch of economics that uses microeconomic techniques to simultaneously determine allocative efficiency within an economy and the income distribution associated with it. It analyzes social welfare, however measured, in terms of economic activities of the individuals that comprise the theoretical society considered. As such, individuals, with associated economic activities, are the basic units for aggregating to social welfare, whether of a group, a community, or a society, and there is no 'social welfare' apart from the 'welfare' associated with its individual units.

a. General equilibrium
c. Tobit model
b. Law of increasing costs
d. Welfare economics

15. In economics, an _____ is a way of representing various distributions of resources. Edgeworth made his presentation in his famous book, Mathematical Psychics: An essay on the application of mathematics to the moral sciences, 1881. Edgeworth's original two axis depiction was developed into the now familiar box diagram by Pareto in 1906 and was popularized in a later exposition by Bowley.

a. International Social Security Association
c. Equivalent variation
b. ACCRA Cost of Living Index
d. Edgeworth box

16. The slope of the production-possibility frontier (PPF) at any given point is called the _____ It describes numerically the rate at which one good can be transformed into the other. It is also called the (marginal) 'opportunity cost' of a commodity, that is, it is the opportunity cost of X in terms of Y at the margin.

a. Piece work
c. Productivity
b. Fordism
d. Marginal rate of transformation

17. In microeconomics, the _____ is the problem consumers face: 'how should I spend my money in order to maximize my utility?'

Suppose their consumption set, or the enumeration of all possible consumption bundles that could be selected if there are no budget constraints has L commodities and is limited to positive amounts of consumption of each

$$x \in \mathbf{R}_+^L .$$

Suppose also that the prices (p) of the L commodities are positive

$$p \in \mathbf{R}_+^L ,$$

and the consumer's wealth is w, then the set of all affordable packages, the budget set, is

$$B(p,w) = \{x \in \mathbf{R}_+^L : \langle p, x \rangle \leq w\} ,$$

Chapter 20. Equilibrium and Time

where $\langle p, x \rangle$ is the inner product of p and x, or the total cost of consuming x of the products at price level p. The consumer would like to buy the best package of commodities it can afford. Suppose that the consumer's utility function (u) is a real valued function with domain of the commodity bundles, or

$$u : \mathbf{R}^L_+ \to \mathbf{R}.$$

Then the consumer's optimal choices x(p, w) are the utility maximizing bundle that is in the budget set, or

$$x(p, w) = \mathrm{argmax}_{x^* \in B(p,w)} u(x^*).$$

a. Utility maximization problem
b. Induced consumption
c. Income elasticity of demand
d. Expenditure minimization problem

18. _____ is an important concept in economics with broad applications in game theory, engineering and the social sciences. The term is named after Vilfredo Pareto, an Italian economist who used the concept in his studies of economic efficiency and income distribution. Informally, pareto efficient situations are those in which any change to make any person better off would make someone else worse off.

a. Pareto efficiency
b. Perfect rationality
c. Lump of labour
d. Matching pennies

19. In economics, a _____ is any economic system that effects its distribution of goods and services with prices and employing any form of money or debt tokens. Except for possible remote and primitive communities, all modern societies use _____s to allocate resources. However, _____s are not used for all resource allocation decisions today.

a. Neomercantilism
b. Price system
c. Hanseatic League
d. Family economy

20. _____ is the a method of technical and economic research of the systems for purpose to optimize a parity between system's consumer functions or properties and expenses to achieve those functions or properties.

This methodology for continuous perfection of production, industrial technologies, organizational structures was developed by Juryj Sobolev in 1948 at the 'Perm telephone factory'

- 1948 Juryj Sobolev - the first success in application of a method analysis at the 'Perm telephone factory'.
- 1949 - the first application for the invention as result of use of the new method.

Chapter 20. Equilibrium and Time

Today in economically developed countries practically each enterprise or the company use methodology of the kind of functional-cost analysis as a practice of the quality management, most full satisfying to principles of standards of series ISO 9000.

- Interest of consumer not in products itself, but the advantage which it will receive from its usage.
- The consumer aspires to reduce his expenses
- Functions needed by consumer can be executed in the various ways, and, hence, with various efficiency and expenses. Among possible alternatives of realization of functions exist such in which the parity of quality and the price is the optimal for the consumer.

The goal of _____ is achievement of the highest consumer satisfaction of production at simultaneous decrease in all kinds of industrial expenses Classical _____ has three English synonyms - Value Engineering, Value Management, Value Analysis.

a. Willingness to pay
c. Monopoly wage
b. Staple financing
d. Function cost analysis

21. Finally, by definition, the optimal decision rule is the one that achieves the best possible value of the objective. For example, if someone chooses consumption, given wealth, in order to maximize happiness (assuming happiness H can be represented by a mathematical function, such as a utility function), then each level of wealth will be associated with some highest possible level of happiness, H(W). The best possible value of the objective, written as a function of the state, is called the _____.

a. Normal equations
c. 100-year flood
b. Linear least squares
d. Value function

22. _____ is a fee paid on borrowed assets. It is the price paid for the use of borrowed money , or, money earned by deposited funds . Assets that are sometimes lent with _____ include money, shares, consumer goods through hire purchase, major assets such as aircraft, and even entire factories in finance lease arrangements.

a. Interest
c. Insolvency
b. Internal debt
d. Asset protection

23. An _____ is the price a borrower pays for the use of money they do not own, for instance a small company might borrow from a bank to kick start their business, and the return a lender receives for deferring the use of funds, by lending it to the borrower. _____s are normally expressed as a percentage rate over the period of one year.

_____s targets are also a vital tool of monetary policy and are used to control variables like investment, inflation, and unemployment.

a. Arrow-Debreu model
c. ACCRA Cost of Living Index
b. Interest rate
d. Enterprise value

Chapter 20. Equilibrium and Time

24. A _____ is:

- Rewrite _____, in generative grammar and computer science
- Standardization, a formal and widely-accepted statement, fact, definition, or qualification
- Operation, a determinate _____ for performing a mathematical operation and obtaining a certain result (Mathematics, Logic)
    - Unary operation
    - Binary operation
- _____ of inference, a function from sets of formulae to formulae (Mathematics, Logic)
- _____ of thumb, principle with broad application that is not intended to be strictly accurate or reliable for every situation. Also often simply referred to as a _____
- Moral, an atomic element of a moral code for guiding choices in human behavior
- Heuristic, a quantized '_____' which shows a tendency or probability for successful function
- A regulation, as in sports
- A Production _____, as in computer science
- Procedural law, a _____ set governing the application of laws to cases
    - A law, which may informally be called a '_____'
    - A court ruling, a decision by a court
- In the U.S. Government, a regulation mandated by Congress, but written or expanded upon by the Executive Branch.
- Norm (sociology), an informal but widely accepted _____, concept, truth, definition, or qualification (social norms, legal norms, coding norms)
- Norm (philosophy), a kind of sentence or a reason to act, feel or believe
- 'Rulership' is the concept of governance by a government:
    - Military _____, governance by a military body
    - Monastic _____, a collection of precepts that guides the life of monks or nuns in a religious order where the superior holds the place of Christ
- Slide _____

- '_____,' a song by Ayumi Hamasaki
- '_____,' a song by rapper Nas
- '_____s,' an album by the band The Whitest Boy Alive
- _____s: Pyaar Ka Superhit Formula, a 2003 Bollywood film
- ruler, an instrument for measuring lengths
- _____, a component of an astrolabe, circumferator or similar instrument
- The _____s, a bestselling self-help book
- _____ Project (Run Up-to-date Linux Everywhere), a project that aims to use up-to-date Linux software on old PCs
- _____ engine, a software system that helps managing business _____s
- Ja _____, a hip hop artist
    - R.U.L.E., a 2005 greatest hits album by rapper Ja _____
- '_____s,' a KMFDM song

a. Demand
b. Rule
c. Procter ' Gamble
d. Technocracy

25. _____ in economics refers to metrics and measures of output from production processes, per unit of input. Labor _____, for example, is typically measured as a ratio of output per labor-hour, an input. _____ may be conceived of as a metrics of the technical or engineering efficiency of production.
- a. Fordism
- b. Production-possibility frontier
- c. Piece work
- d. Productivity

26. In economics, a _____ is a function that specifies the output of a firm, an industry, or an entire economy for all combinations of inputs. A meta-_____ compares the practice of the existing entities converting inputs X into output y to determine the most efficient practice _____ of the existing entities, whether the most efficient feasible practice production or the most efficient actual practice production. In either case, the maximum output of a technologically-determined production process is a mathematical function of input factors of production.
- a. Post-Fordism
- b. Production function
- c. Short-run
- d. Constant elasticity of substitution

27. The _____ is a result in General equilibrium economics. It states that the system of excess demand functions for an economy is not restricted by the usual rationality restrictions on individual demands in the economy. Thus microeconomic rationality assumptions have no equivalent macroeconomic implications.
- a. Quantity adjustment
- b. Regular economy
- c. Sonnenschein-Mantel-Debreu theorem
- d. Differential tax analysis

28. A _____ is an object whose consumption increases the utility of the consumer, for which the quantity demanded exceeds the quantity supplied at zero price. _____s are usually modeled as having diminishing marginal utility. The first individual purchase has high utility; the second has less.
- a. Composite good
- b. Merit good
- c. Pie method
- d. Good

29. _____s are financial contracts whose values are derived from the value of something else (known as the underlying.) The underlying value on which a _____ is based can be an asset (e.g., commodities, equities (stocks), residential mortgages, commercial real estate, loans, bonds), an index (e.g., interest rates, exchange rates, stock market indices, consumer price index (CPI) -- see inflation _____s), weather conditions bonds or other forms of credit.
- a. Derivative
- b. 100-year flood
- c. 130-30 fund
- d. Second derivative

30. In microeconomic theory a preference map or _____ is the collection of indifference curves possessed by an individual. Similar in nature to a topographical map, the contour lines of such a map demonstrating progressively more desirable options as they move upward or to the right. Because of the nature of indifference curves they cannot intersect and are effectively infinite in number, their sum defining all possible combinations of values.
- a. Elasticity of substitution
- b. Expenditure minimization problem
- c. Engel curve
- d. Indifference map

31. _____ is a broad label that refers to any individuals or households that use goods and services generated within the economy. The concept of a _____ is used in different contexts, so that the usage and significance of the term may vary.

Chapter 20. Equilibrium and Time

Typically when business people and economists talk of _____s they are talking about person as _____, an aggregated commodity item with little individuality other than that expressed in the buy/not-buy decision.

a. 100-year flood
c. 1921 recession
b. 130-30 fund
d. Consumer

32. Competitive market equilibrium is the traditional concept of economic equilibrium, appropriate for the analysis of commodity markets with flexible prices and many traders, and serving as the benchmark of efficiency in economic analysis. It relies crucially on the assumption of a competitive environment where each trader decides upon a quantity that is so small compared to the total quantity traded in the market that their individual transactions have no influence on the prices.Competitive markets are an ideal, a standard that other market structures are evaluated by.

A _____ consists of a vector of prices and an allocation such that given the prices, each trader by maximizing his objective function (profit, preferences) subject to his technological possibilities and resource constraints plans to trade into his part of the proposed allocation, and such that the prices make all net trades compatible with one another ('clear the market') by equating aggregate supply and demand for the commodities which are traded.

a. Product-Market Growth Matrix
c. Market system
b. Partial equilibrium
d. Competitive equilibrium

33. A _____ represents the combinations of goods and services that a consumer can purchase given current prices and his income. Consumer theory uses the concepts of a _____ and a preference map to analyze consumer choices. Both concepts have a ready graphical representation in the two-good case.

a. Joint demand
c. Quality bias
b. Revealed preference
d. Budget constraint

34. There are two _____. The first states that any competitive equilibrium or Walrasian equilibrium leads to a Pareto efficient allocation of resources. The second states the converse, that any efficient allocation can be sustainable by a competitive equilibrium.

a. Stolper-Samuelson theorem
c. 100-year flood
b. No-trade theorem
d. Fundamental theorems of welfare economics

Chapter 20. Equilibrium and Time

35. Economics:

    - _____,the desire to own something and the ability to pay for it
    - _____ curve,a graphic representation of a _____ schedule
    - _____ deposit, the money in checking accounts
    - _____ pull theory,the theory that inflation occurs when _____ for goods and services exceeds existing supplies
    - _____ schedule,a table that lists the quantity of a good a person will buy it each different price
    - _____ side economics,the school of economics at believes government spending and tax cuts open economy by raising _____

    a. Variability
    c. Production
    b. McKesson ' Robbins scandal
    d. Demand

36. In economics, _____ is when quantity demanded is more than quantity supplied.See Economic shortage.
    a. ACCRA Cost of Living Index
    b. Excess demand
    c. AD-IA Model
    d. ACEA agreement

37. In economics, the _____ is an economic law that states that consumers buy more of a good when its price decreases and less when its price increases.

    There are certain goods which do not follow this law. These include Veblen and Giffen goods

    a. Financial crisis
    c. Market failure
    b. Georgism
    d. Law of demand

38. An _____, abbreviated to OLG model, is a type of economic model in which agents live a finite length of time and live long enough to endure into at least one period of the next generation's lives.

    The concept of an OLG model was devised by Maurice Allais in 1947 and popularized by Paul Samuelson in 1958 as a way of simplifing monetary economics and macroeconomic models. OLG models can have varying characteristics depending on the subject of study, but most models share several key elements:

    - individuals receive an endowment of goods at birth
    - goods cannot endure for more than one period
    - money endures for multiple periods
    - individuals must consume in all periods, and their lifetime utility is a function of consumption in all periods

    The most basic OLG model has the following characteristics:

    - Individuals live for two periods; in the first period of life, they are referred to as the Young. In the second period of life, they are referred to as the Old.

a. Adam Smith
c. Adolph Fischer
b. Adolf Hitler
d. Overlapping generations model

39. In social choice theory, Arrow's _____ demonstrates that no voting system can convert the ranked preferences of individuals into a community-wide ranking while also meeting a certain set of reasonable criteria with three or more discrete options to choose from. These criteria are called unrestricted domain, non-imposition, non-dictatorship, Pareto efficiency, and independence of irrelevant alternatives. The theorem is often cited in discussions of election theory as it is further interpreted by the Gibbard-Satterthwaite theorem.

a. Impossibility theorem
c. ACCRA Cost of Living Index
b. AD-IA Model
d. ACEA agreement

Chapter 21. Social Choice Theory

1. In probability theory and statistics, a _____ is described as the number separating the higher half of a sample, a population from the lower half. The _____ of a finite list of numbers can be found by arranging all the observations from lowest value to highest value and picking the middle one. If there is an even number of observations, the _____ is not unique, so one often takes the mean of the two middle values.
   - a. Labour vouchers
   - b. First player wins
   - c. Median
   - d. Fiscal stimulus plans

2. _____ studies how measures of individual interests, values, or welfares in theory could be aggregated to reach a collective decision. A non-theoretical example of a collective decision is passing a set of laws under a constitution. _____ dates from Condorcet's formulation of the voting paradox.
   - a. Social choice theory
   - b. 1921 recession
   - c. 130-30 fund
   - d. 100-year flood

3. In social choice theory, Arrow's _____ demonstrates that no voting system can convert the ranked preferences of individuals into a community-wide ranking while also meeting a certain set of reasonable criteria with three or more discrete options to choose from. These criteria are called unrestricted domain, non-imposition, non-dictatorship, Pareto efficiency, and independence of irrelevant alternatives. The theorem is often cited in discussions of election theory as it is further interpreted by the Gibbard-Satterthwaite theorem.
   - a. ACEA agreement
   - b. Impossibility theorem
   - c. AD-IA Model
   - d. ACCRA Cost of Living Index

4. A _____ provision refers to any program which seeks to provide a minimum level of income, service or other support for many marginalized groups such as the poor, elderly, and disabled people. _____ programs are undertaken by governments as well as non-governmental organizations (NGOs.) _____ payments and services are typically provided at the expense of taxpayers generally, funded by benefactors, or by compulsory enrollment of the poor themselves.
   - a. 1921 recession
   - b. 100-year flood
   - c. Social welfare
   - d. 130-30 fund

5. The _____ is the apparent contradiction that although water is on the whole more useful, in terms of survival, than diamonds, diamonds command a higher price in the market. The economist Adam Smith is often considered to be the classic presenter of this paradox. Nicolaus Copernicus, John Locke, John Law and others had previously tried to explain the disparity.
   - a. 100-year flood
   - b. St. Petersburg paradox
   - c. 130-30 fund
   - d. Paradox of value

6. In finance, _____ is a measure of the sensitivity of the duration of a bond to changes in interest rates. There is an inverse relationship between _____ and sensitivity - in general, the higher the _____ less sensitive the bond price is to interest rate shifts, the lower the _____, the more sensitive it is.

Duration is a linear measure or 1st derivative of how the price of a bond changes in response to interest rate changes.

   - a. Convexity
   - b. Russian financial crisis
   - c. Rule
   - d. Technocracy

Chapter 21. Social Choice Theory

7. In calculus, a function f defined on a subset of the real numbers with real values is called _____, if for all x and y such that x >≤ y one has f(x) >≤ f(y), so f preserves the order. In layman's terms, the sign of the slope is always positive (the curve tending upwards) or zero (i.e., non-decreasing, or asymptotic, or depicted as a horizontal, flat line) Likewise, a function is called monotonically decreasing (non-increasing) if, whenever x >≤ y, then f(x) >≥ f(y), so it reverses the order.
   a. 100-year flood
   b. 1921 recession
   c. 130-30 fund
   d. Monotonic

8. _____ refers to methods in probability and statistics named after the Reverend Thomas Bayes (ca. 1702-1761), in particular methods related to:

   - the degree-of-belief interpretation of probability, as opposed to frequency or proportion or propensity interpretations; or
   - Bayes' theorem on conditional probability.

   These methods include:

   - Bayes estimator
   - Bayes factor
   - _____ average
   - _____ spam filtering
   - _____ game
   - _____ inference
   - _____ information criterion
   - _____ multivariate linear regression
     o _____ linear regression, a special case
   - _____ model comparison
   - _____ network
   - _____ probability
   - Empirical Bayes method
   - Naive Bayes classifier

   _____ also refers to the application of this probability theory to the functioning of the brain

   - _____ brain

   a. Technocracy
   b. Fiscal
   c. Bayesian
   d. Freedom Park

9. In economics and sociology, an _____ is any factor (financial or non-financial) that enables or motivates a particular course of action, or counts as a reason for preferring one choice to the alternatives. It is an expectation that encourages people to behave in a certain way. Since human beings are purposeful creatures, the study of _____ structures is central to the study of all economic activity (both in terms of individual decision-making and in terms of co-operation and competition within a larger institutional structure.)

a. Isocost
b. Economic reform
c. Epstein-Zin preferences
d. Incentive

10. To _____ is to impose a financial charge or other levy upon a taxpayer by a state or the functional equivalent of a state.

_____es are also imposed by many subnational entities. _____es consist of direct _____ or indirect _____, and may be paid in money or as its labour equivalent (often but not always unpaid.)

a. 130-30 fund
b. 100-year flood
c. 1921 recession
d. Tax

Chapter 22. Elements of Welfare Economics and Axiomatic Bargaining

1. _____ is a branch of economics that uses microeconomic techniques to simultaneously determine allocative efficiency within an economy and the income distribution associated with it. It analyzes social welfare, however measured, in terms of economic activities of the individuals that comprise the theoretical society considered. As such, individuals, with associated economic activities, are the basic units for aggregating to social welfare, whether of a group, a community, or a society, and there is no 'social welfare' apart from the 'welfare' associated with its individual units.
   a. Law of increasing costs
   b. General equilibrium
   c. Tobit model
   d. Welfare economics

2. _____s is the social science that studies the production, distribution, and consumption of goods and services. The term _____s comes from the Ancient Greek oá¼°κονομῖα from oá¼¶κος (oikos, 'house') + νἴŒμος (nomos, 'custom' or 'law'), hence 'rules of the house(hold)'. Current _____ models developed out of the broader field of political economy in the late 19th century, owing to a desire to use an empirical approach more akin to the physical sciences.
   a. Energy economics
   b. Inflation
   c. Opportunity cost
   d. Economic

3. _____ is an important concept in economics with broad applications in game theory, engineering and the social sciences. The term is named after Vilfredo Pareto, an Italian economist who used the concept in his studies of economic efficiency and income distribution. Informally, pareto efficient situations are those in which any change to make any person better off would make someone else worse off.
   a. Lump of labour
   b. Matching pennies
   c. Perfect rationality
   d. Pareto efficiency

4. In economics, _____ is a measure of the relative satisfaction from consumption of various goods and services. Given this measure, one may speak meaningfully of increasing or decreasing _____, and thereby explain economic behavior in terms of attempts to increase one's _____. For illustrative purposes, changes in _____ are sometimes expressed in units called utils.
   a. Utility function
   b. Expected utility hypothesis
   c. Utility
   d. Ordinal utility

5. In economics, _____ is the total demand for final goods and services in the economy (Y) at a given time and price level. It is the amount of goods and services in the economy that will be purchased at all possible price levels. This is the demand for the gross domestic product of a country when inventory levels are static.
   a. Aggregation problem
   b. Aggregate supply
   c. Aggregate expenditure
   d. Aggregate demand

6. Economics:

   - _____,the desire to own something and the ability to pay for it
   - _____ curve,a graphic representation of a _____ schedule
   - _____ deposit, the money in checking accounts
   - _____ pull theory,the theory that inflation occurs when _____ for goods and services exceeds existing supplies
   - _____ schedule,a table that lists the quantity of a good a person will buy it each different price
   - _____ side economics,the school of economics at believes government spending and tax cuts open economy by raising _____

a. Variability
b. Demand
c. Production
d. McKesson ' Robbins scandal

7. A _____ is something for which there is demand, but which is supplied without qualitative differentiation across a market. It is a product that is the same no matter who produces it, such as petroleum, notebook paper, or milk. In other words, copper is copper.
   a. Hard commodity
   b. Soft commodity
   c. 100-year flood
   d. Commodity

8. A _____ provision refers to any program which seeks to provide a minimum level of income, service or other support for many marginalized groups such as the poor, elderly, and disabled people. _____ programs are undertaken by governments as well as non-governmental organizations (NGOs.) _____ payments and services are typically provided at the expense of taxpayers generally, funded by benefactors, or by compulsory enrollment of the poor themselves.
   a. 100-year flood
   b. 130-30 fund
   c. 1921 recession
   d. Social welfare

9. In economics, a _____ is a real-valued function that ranks conceivable social states (alternative complete descriptions of the society) from lowest to highest. Inputs of the function include any variables considered to affect welfare of the society (Sen, 1970, p. 33.)
   a. Contract curve
   b. Gini coefficient
   c. Frisch elasticity of labor supply
   d. Social welfare function

10. In mathematics, an _____ is a statement about the relative size or order of two objects, or about whether they are the same or not

- The notation a < b means that a is less than b.
- The notation a > b means that a is greater than b.
- The notation a ≠ b means that a is not equal to b, but does not say that one is greater than the other or even that they can be compared in size.

In each statement above, a is not equal to b. These relations are known as strict inequalities. The notation a < b may also be read as 'a is strictly less than b'.

   a. ACEA agreement
   b. ACCRA Cost of Living Index
   c. AD-IA Model
   d. Inequality

11. _____ is a concept in economics, finance, and psychology related to the behaviour of consumers and investors under uncertainty. _____ is the reluctance of a person to accept a bargain with an uncertain payoff rather than another bargain with a more certain, but possibly lower, expected payoff. For example, a risk-averse investor might choose to put his or her money into a bank account with a low but guaranteed interest rate, rather than into a stock that is likely to have high returns, but also has a chance of becoming worthless.
   a. Risk theory
   b. Compound annual growth rate
   c. Reinsurance
   d. Risk aversion

Chapter 22. Elements of Welfare Economics and Axiomatic Bargaining

12. A _____ is:

   - Rewrite _____, in generative grammar and computer science
   - Standardization, a formal and widely-accepted statement, fact, definition, or qualification
   - Operation, a determinate _____ for performing a mathematical operation and obtaining a certain result (Mathematics, Logic)
     - Unary operation
     - Binary operation
   - _____ of inference, a function from sets of formulae to formulae (Mathematics, Logic)
   - _____ of thumb, principle with broad application that is not intended to be strictly accurate or reliable for every situation. Also often simply referred to as a _____
   - Moral, an atomic element of a moral code for guiding choices in human behavior
   - Heuristic, a quantized '_____' which shows a tendency or probability for successful function
   - A regulation, as in sports
   - A Production _____, as in computer science
   - Procedural law, a _____ set governing the application of laws to cases
     - A law, which may informally be called a '_____'
     - A court ruling, a decision by a court
   - In the U.S. Government, a regulation mandated by Congress, but written or expanded upon by the Executive Branch.
   - Norm (sociology), an informal but widely accepted _____, concept, truth, definition, or qualification (social norms, legal norms, coding norms)
   - Norm (philosophy), a kind of sentence or a reason to act, feel or believe
   - 'Rulership' is the concept of governance by a government:
     - Military _____, governance by a military body
     - Monastic _____, a collection of precepts that guides the life of monks or nuns in a religious order where the superior holds the place of Christ
   - Slide _____

   - '_____,' a song by Ayumi Hamasaki
   - '_____,' a song by rapper Nas
   - '_____s,' an album by the band The Whitest Boy Alive
   - _____s: Pyaar Ka Superhit Formula, a 2003 Bollywood film
   - ruler, an instrument for measuring lengths
   - _____, a component of an astrolabe, circumferator or similar instrument
   - The _____s, a bestselling self-help book
   - _____ Project (Run Up-to-date Linux Everywhere), a project that aims to use up-to-date Linux software on old PCs
   - _____ engine, a software system that helps managing business _____s
   - Ja _____, a hip hop artist
     - R.U.L.E., a 2005 greatest hits album by rapper Ja _____
   - '_____s,' a KMFDM song

a. Procter ' Gamble
b. Technocracy
c. Demand
d. Rule

Chapter 22. Elements of Welfare Economics and Axiomatic Bargaining

13. In economics, _____ is the ratio of the percent change in one variable to the percent change in another variable. It is a tool for measuring the responsiveness of a function to changes in parameters in a relative way. Commonly analyzed are _____ of substitution, price and wealth.
    a. Elasticity of demand
    b. ACCRA Cost of Living Index
    c. Elasticity
    d. ACEA agreement

14. In welfare economics, the _____ refers to a decision rule used to select between pairs of alternative feasible social states. One of these states is the hypothetical point of departure ('the original state'.) According to the _____, if the prospective gainers could compensate (any) prospective losers and leave no one worse off, the other state is to be selected (Chipman, 1987, p.
    a. Missing market
    b. Triple bottom line
    c. Compensation principle
    d. Structural adjustment loan

15. _____ is the a method of technical and economic research of the systems for purpose to optimize a parity between system's consumer functions or properties and expenses to achieve those functions or properties.

This methodology for continuous perfection of production, industrial technologies, organizational structures was developed by Juryj Sobolev in 1948 at the 'Perm telephone factory'

- 1948 Juryj Sobolev - the first success in application of a method analysis at the 'Perm telephone factory' .
- 1949 - the first application for the invention as result of use of the new method.

Today in economically developed countries practically each enterprise or the company use methodology of the kind of functional-cost analysis as a practice of the quality management, most full satisfying to principles of standards of series ISO 9000.

- Interest of consumer not in products itself, but the advantage which it will receive from its usage.
- The consumer aspires to reduce his expenses
- Functions needed by consumer can be executed in the various ways, and, hence, with various efficiency and expenses. Among possible alternatives of realization of functions exist such in which the parity of quality and the price is the optimal for the consumer.

The goal of _____ is achievement of the highest consumer satisfaction of production at simultaneous decrease in all kinds of industrial expenses Classical _____ has three English synonyms - Value Engineering, Value Management, Value Analysis.

    a. Staple financing
    b. Willingness to pay
    c. Monopoly wage
    d. Function cost analysis

16. In calculus, a function f defined on a subset of the real numbers with real values is called _____, if for all x and y such that x >≤ y one has f(x) >≤ f(y), so f preserves the order. In layman's terms, the sign of the slope is always positive (the curve tending upwards) or zero (i.e., non-decreasing, or asymptotic, or depicted as a horizontal, flat line) Likewise, a function is called monotonically decreasing (non-increasing) if, whenever x >≤ y, then f(x) >≥ f(y), so it reverses the order.

Chapter 22. Elements of Welfare Economics and Axiomatic Bargaining

a. 130-30 fund
c. Monotonic
b. 100-year flood
d. 1921 recession

17. In social choice theory, Arrow's _____ demonstrates that no voting system can convert the ranked preferences of individuals into a community-wide ranking while also meeting a certain set of reasonable criteria with three or more discrete options to choose from. These criteria are called unrestricted domain, non-imposition, non-dictatorship, Pareto efficiency, and independence of irrelevant alternatives. The theorem is often cited in discussions of election theory as it is further interpreted by the Gibbard-Satterthwaite theorem.

a. ACEA agreement
c. ACCRA Cost of Living Index
b. Impossibility theorem
d. AD-IA Model

18. A _____ proof is a mathematical proof that a particular theory is consistent. The early development of mathematical proof theory was driven by the desire to provide finitary _____ proofs for all of mathematics as part of Hilbert's program. Hilbert's program was strongly impacted by incompleteness theorems, which showed that sufficiently strong proof theories cannot prove their own _____.

a. Consistency
c. Reason
b. 130-30 fund
d. 100-year flood

19. _____ has several particular meanings:

- in mathematics
    - _____ function
    - Euler _____
    - _____
    - _____ subgroup
    - method of _____s (partial differential equations)
- in physics and engineering
    - any _____ curve that shows the relationship between certain input- and output parameters, e.g.
    - an I-V or current-voltage _____ is the current in a circuit as a function of the applied voltage
    - Receiver-Operator _____
- in fiction
    - in Dungeons ' Dragons, _____ is another name for ability score

a. Characteristic
c. Russian financial crisis
b. Technocracy
d. Demand

20. In game theory, a _____, named in honour of Lloyd Shapley, who introduced it in 1953, describes one approach to the fair allocation of gains obtained by cooperation among several actors.

The setup is as follows: a coalition of actors cooperates, and obtains a certain overall gain from that cooperation. Since some actors may contribute more to the coalition than others, the question arises how to distribute fairly the gains among the actors.

a. Fictitious play
c. Smart market
b. Markov perfect
d. Shapley value

21. While preferences are the conventional foundation of microeconomics, it is often convenient to represent preferences with a _____ and reason indirectly about preferences with _____s. Let X be the consumption set, the set of all mutually-exclusive packages the consumer could conceivably consume (such as an indifference curve map without the indifference curves.) The consumer's _____ $u : X \to \mathbf{R}$ ranks each package in the consumption set.
   a. Ordinal utility
   c. Expected utility hypothesis
   b. Utility function
   d. Utility

Chapter 23. Incentives and Mechanism Design

1. The _____ of economics can be stated as, 'To any Bayesian Nash equilibrium of a game of incomplete information, there corresponds an associated revelation mechanism that has an equilibrium where the players truthfully report their types.'

For dominant strategies, instead of Bayesian equilibrium, the _____ was introduced by Gibbard (1973.) Later this principle was extended to the broader solution concept of Bayesian equilibrium by Dasgupta, Hammond and Maskin (1979), Holmstrom (1977), and Myerson (1979.)

The _____ is useful in game theory, Mechanism design, social welfare and auctions.

a. 100-year flood   b. X-efficiency
c. X-inefficiency   d. Revelation principle

2. _____ refers to methods in probability and statistics named after the Reverend Thomas Bayes (ca. 1702-1761), in particular methods related to:

- the degree-of-belief interpretation of probability, as opposed to frequency or proportion or propensity interpretations; or
- Bayes' theorem on conditional probability.

These methods include:

- Bayes estimator
- Bayes factor
- _____ average
- _____ spam filtering
- _____ game
- _____ inference
- _____ information criterion
- _____ multivariate linear regression
  - _____ linear regression, a special case
- _____ model comparison
- _____ network
- _____ probability
- Empirical Bayes method
- Naive Bayes classifier

_____ also refers to the application of this probability theory to the functioning of the brain

- _____ brain

a. Fiscal   b. Technocracy
c. Freedom Park   d. Bayesian

Chapter 23. Incentives and Mechanism Design

3. _____ is a term used in economics and game theory to describe an economic situation or game in which knowledge about other market participants or players is available to all participants. Every player knows the payoffs and strategies available to other players.

   _____ is one of the theoretical pre-conditions of an efficient perfectly competitive market.

   a. Replicator equation
   b. Repeated game
   c. Metagame analysis
   d. Complete information

4. The _____ is an important result in mechanism design and the economics of asymmetric information. Informally, the result says that there is no efficient way for two parties to trade a good when they each have secret and probabilistically varying valuations for it, without the risk of forcing one party to trade at a loss.

   Formally, the theorem applies if a prospective buyer A has a valuation $v_A \in [x_a, y_a]$, and the prospective seller B has an independent valuation $v_B \in [x_b, y_b]$, such that the intervals $[x_a, y_a]$ and $[x_b, y_b]$ overlap, and the probability densities for the valuations are strictly positive on those intervals.

   a. 130-30 fund
   b. 100-year flood
   c. 1921 recession
   d. Myerson-Satterthwaite theorem

5. In game theory, _____ is a solution concept of a game involving two or more players, in which each player is assumed to know the equilibrium strategies of the other players, and no player has anything to gain by changing only his or her own strategy unilaterally. If each player has chosen a strategy and no player can benefit by changing his or her strategy while the other players keep theirs unchanged, then the current set of strategy choices and the corresponding payoffs constitute a _____.

   Stated simply, Amy and Bill are in _____ if Amy is making the best decision she can, taking into account Bill's decision, and Bill is making the best decision he can, taking into account Amy's decision.

   a. Lump of labour
   b. Linear production game
   c. Nash equilibrium
   d. Proper equilibrium

6. In economics, _____ is a measure of the relative satisfaction from consumption of various goods and services. Given this measure, one may speak meaningfully of increasing or decreasing _____, and thereby explain economic behavior in terms of attempts to increase one's _____. For illustrative purposes, changes in _____ are sometimes expressed in units called utils.

   a. Expected utility hypothesis
   b. Ordinal utility
   c. Utility
   d. Utility function

7. While preferences are the conventional foundation of microeconomics, it is often convenient to represent preferences with a _____ and reason indirectly about preferences with _____s. Let X be the consumption set, the set of all mutually-exclusive packages the consumer could conceivably consume (such as an indifference curve map without the indifference curves.) The consumer's _____ $u : X \to \mathbf{R}$ ranks each package in the consumption set.

a. Utility function
b. Ordinal utility
c. Expected utility hypothesis
d. Utility

8. In economics, the _____ is the change in consumption resulting from a change in real income.

Another important item that can change is the money income of the consumer. The _____ is the phenomenon observed through changes in purchasing power.

a. Export subsidy
b. Equilibrium wage
c. Inflation hedge
d. Income effect

9. _____ studies how measures of individual interests, values, or welfares in theory could be aggregated to reach a collective decision. A non-theoretical example of a collective decision is passing a set of laws under a constitution. _____ dates from Condorcet's formulation of the voting paradox.

a. Social choice theory
b. 100-year flood
c. 130-30 fund
d. 1921 recession

10. A _____ provision refers to any program which seeks to provide a minimum level of income, service or other support for many marginalized groups such as the poor, elderly, and disabled people. _____ programs are undertaken by governments as well as non-governmental organizations (NGOs.) _____ payments and services are typically provided at the expense of taxpayers generally, funded by benefactors, or by compulsory enrollment of the poor themselves.

a. Social welfare
b. 1921 recession
c. 100-year flood
d. 130-30 fund

11. In economics, a _____ is a real-valued function that ranks conceivable social states (alternative complete descriptions of the society) from lowest to highest. Inputs of the function include any variables considered to affect welfare of the society (Sen, 1970, p. 33.)

a. Social welfare function
b. Gini coefficient
c. Contract curve
d. Frisch elasticity of labor supply

12. _____ is the a method of technical and economic research of the systems for purpose to optimize a parity between system's consumer functions or properties and expenses to achieve those functions or properties.

This methodology for continuous perfection of production, industrial technologies, organizational structures was developed by Juryj Sobolev in 1948 at the 'Perm telephone factory'

- 1948 Juryj Sobolev - the first success in application of a method analysis at the 'Perm telephone factory' .
- 1949 - the first application for the invention as result of use of the new method.

Chapter 23. Incentives and Mechanism Design

Today in economically developed countries practically each enterprise or the company use methodology of the kind of functional-cost analysis as a practice of the quality management, most full satisfying to principles of standards of series ISO 9000.

- Interest of consumer not in products itself, but the advantage which it will receive from its usage.
- The consumer aspires to reduce his expenses
- Functions needed by consumer can be executed in the various ways, and, hence, with various efficiency and expenses. Among possible alternatives of realization of functions exist such in which the parity of quality and the price is the optimal for the consumer.

The goal of _____ is achievement of the highest consumer satisfaction of production at simultaneous decrease in all kinds of industrial expenses Classical _____ has three English synonyms - Value Engineering, Value Management, Value Analysis.

a. Staple financing
c. Willingness to pay
b. Monopoly wage
d. Function cost analysis

13. In economics and sociology, an _____ is any factor (financial or non-financial) that enables or motivates a particular course of action, or counts as a reason for preferring one choice to the alternatives. It is an expectation that encourages people to behave in a certain way. Since human beings are purposeful creatures, the study of _____ structures is central to the study of all economic activity (both in terms of individual decision-making and in terms of co-operation and competition within a larger institutional structure.)

a. Incentive
c. Epstein-Zin preferences
b. Isocost
d. Economic reform

14. _____ refers to the movement of cash into or out of a business or financial product. It is usually measured during a specified, finite period of time. Measurement of _____ can be used

- to determine a project's rate of return or value. The time of _____s into and out of projects are used as inputs in financial models such as internal rate of return, and net present value.
- to determine problems with a business's liquidity. Being profitable does not necessarily mean being liquid. A company can fail because of a shortage of cash, even while profitable.
- as an alternate measure of a business's profits when it is believed that accrual accounting concepts do not represent economic realities. For example, a company may be notionally profitable but generating little operational cash (as may be the case for a company that barters its products rather than selling for cash.) In such a case, the company may be deriving additional operating cash by issuing shares evaluating default risk, re-investment requirements, etc.

_____ is a generic term used differently depending on the context. It may be defined by users for their own purposes.

a. Second lien loan
c. Restricted stock
b. Strip financing
d. Cash flow

Chapter 23. Incentives and Mechanism Design 139

15. A _____ is:

- Rewrite _____, in generative grammar and computer science
- Standardization, a formal and widely-accepted statement, fact, definition, or qualification
- Operation, a determinate _____ for performing a mathematical operation and obtaining a certain result (Mathematics, Logic)
    - Unary operation
    - Binary operation
- _____ of inference, a function from sets of formulae to formulae (Mathematics, Logic)
- _____ of thumb, principle with broad application that is not intended to be strictly accurate or reliable for every situation. Also often simply referred to as a _____
- Moral, an atomic element of a moral code for guiding choices in human behavior
- Heuristic, a quantized '_____' which shows a tendency or probability for successful function
- A regulation, as in sports
- A Production _____, as in computer science
- Procedural law, a _____ set governing the application of laws to cases
    - A law, which may informally be called a '_____'
    - A court ruling, a decision by a court
- In the U.S. Government, a regulation mandated by Congress, but written or expanded upon by the Executive Branch.
- Norm (sociology), an informal but widely accepted _____, concept, truth, definition, or qualification (social norms, legal norms, coding norms)
- Norm (philosophy), a kind of sentence or a reason to act, feel or believe
- 'Rulership' is the concept of governance by a government:
    - Military _____, governance by a military body
    - Monastic _____, a collection of precepts that guides the life of monks or nuns in a religious order where the superior holds the place of Christ
- Slide _____

- '_____,' a song by Ayumi Hamasaki
- '_____,' a song by rapper Nas
- '_____s,' an album by the band The Whitest Boy Alive
- _____s: Pyaar Ka Superhit Formula, a 2003 Bollywood film
- ruler, an instrument for measuring lengths
- _____, a component of an astrolabe, circumferator or similar instrument
- The _____s, a bestselling self-help book
- _____ Project (Run Up-to-date Linux Everywhere), a project that aims to use up-to-date Linux software on old PCs
- _____ engine, a software system that helps managing business _____s
- Ja _____, a hip hop artist
    - R.U.L.E., a 2005 greatest hits album by rapper Ja _____
- '_____s,' a KMFDM song

a. Procter ' Gamble
c. Demand
b. Rule
d. Technocracy

Chapter 23. Incentives and Mechanism Design

16. A _____ is an object whose consumption increases the utility of the consumer, for which the quantity demanded exceeds the quantity supplied at zero price. _____s are usually modeled as having diminishing marginal utility. The first individual purchase has high utility; the second has less.
   a. Good
   b. Pie method
   c. Merit good
   d. Composite good

17. A _____ is defined in economics as a good that exhibits these properties:

   - Excludable - it is reasonably possible to prevent a class of consumers (e.g. those who have not paid for it) from consuming the good.
   - Rivalrous - consumptions by one consumer prevents simultaneous consumption by other consumers. _____s satisfies an individual want while public good satisfies a collective want of the society.

   A _____ is the opposite of a public good, as they are almost exclusively made for profit.

   An example of the _____ is bread: bread eaten by a given person cannot be consumed by another (rivalry), and it is easy for a baker to refuse to trade a loaf (excludable

   a. Positional goods
   b. Pie method
   c. Demerit good
   d. Private good

18. _____ or clearing trade is trade exclusively between two states, particularly, barter trade based on bilateral deals between governments, and without using hard currency for payment. _____ agreements often aim to keep trade deficits at minimum by keeping a clearing account where deficit would accumulate.

   The Soviet Union conducted _____ with two nations, India and Finland.

   a. 130-30 fund
   b. 1921 recession
   c. 100-year flood
   d. Bilateral trade

19. A _____ is a form of auction where bidders submit one bid in a concealed fashion. The submitted bids are then compared and the person with the highest bid wins the award, and pays the amount of his bid to the seller. This differs from a standard English auction in that bids are not open or called; bidders must submit valuations based upon supposed market value and their own willingness to pay -- as opposed to engaging in competition through relative prices with other bidders.
   a. First-price sealed-bid auction
   b. Capital surplus
   c. Financial result
   d. Flight-to-liquidity

20. A _____ is a type of sealed-bid auction, where bidders submit written bids without knowing the bid of the other people in the auction. The highest bidder wins, but the price paid is the second-highest bid. The auction was created by William Vickrey.
   a. Forward auction
   b. Mystery auction
   c. Box social
   d. Vickrey auction

Chapter 23. Incentives and Mechanism Design

21. In game theory, a _____ is one in which information about characteristics of the other players (i.e. payoffs) is incomplete. Following John C. Harsanyi's framework, a _____ can be modelled by introducing Nature as a player in a game. Nature assigns a random variable to each player which could take values of types for each player and associating probabilities or a probability density function with those types (in the course of the game, nature randomly chooses a type for each player according to the probability distribution across each player's type space.)
    a. Strong prior
    b. Sparse binary polynomial hashing
    c. Random naive Bayes
    d. Bayesian game

22. In calculus, a function f defined on a subset of the real numbers with real values is called _____, if for all x and y such that x >≤ y one has f(x) >≤ f(y), so f preserves the order. In layman's terms, the sign of the slope is always positive (the curve tending upwards) or zero (i.e., non-decreasing, or asymptotic, or depicted as a horizontal, flat line) Likewise, a function is called monotonically decreasing (non-increasing) if, whenever x >≤ y, then f(x) >≥ f(y), so it reverses the order.
    a. Monotonic
    b. 100-year flood
    c. 1921 recession
    d. 130-30 fund

23. In economics, an _____ or spillover of an economic transaction is an impact on a party that is not directly involved in the transaction. In such a case, prices do not reflect the full costs or benefits in production or consumption of a product or service. A positive impact is called an external benefit, while a negative impact is called an external cost.
    a. Environmental impact assessment
    b. Existence value
    c. Environmental tariff
    d. Externality

24. In mechanism design, a process is said to be incentive compatible if all of the participants fare best when they truthfully reveal any private information asked for by the mechanism. As an illustration, voting systems which create incentives to vote dishonestly lack the property of _____. In the absence of dummy bidders or collusion, a second price auction is an example of mechanism that is incentive compatible.
    a. AD-IA Model
    b. ACEA agreement
    c. ACCRA Cost of Living Index
    d. Incentive compatibility

25. The term _____ is a neo-Latin word meaning 'before the event'. _____ is used most commonly in the commercial world, where results of a particular action, or series of actions, are forecast in advance. The opposite of _____ is ex-post.
    a. ACCRA Cost of Living Index
    b. Ex-ante
    c. AD-IA Model
    d. ACEA agreement

26. In economics, game theory, and decision theory the _____ theorem or _____ hypothesis predicts that the 'betting preferences' of people with regard to uncertain outcomes (gambles) can be described by a mathematical relation which takes into account the size of a payout (whether in money or other goods), the probability of occurrence, risk aversion, and the different utility of the same payout to people with different assets or personal preferences. It is a more sophisticated theory than simply predicting that choices will be made based on expected value (which takes into account only the size of the payout and the probability of occurrence.)

Daniel Bernoulli described the complete theory in 1738.

    a. Utility
    b. Ordinal utility
    c. Expected utility
    d. Expected utility hypothesis

Chapter 23. Incentives and Mechanism Design

27. _____ is an important concept in economics with broad applications in game theory, engineering and the social sciences. The term is named after Vilfredo Pareto, an Italian economist who used the concept in his studies of economic efficiency and income distribution. Informally, pareto efficient situations are those in which any change to make any person better off would make someone else worse off.

   a. Matching pennies
   b. Lump of labour
   c. Perfect rationality
   d. Pareto efficiency

28. Economic _____ is defined as an excess distribution to any factor in a production process above that which is required to induce the factor into the process or any excess above that which is necessary to keep the factor in its current use..

   Classical Factor _____ is primarily concerned with the fee paid for the use of fixed (e.g. natural) resources. The classical definition is expressed as any excess payment above that required to induce or provide for production.

   a. Rent
   b. 1921 recession
   c. 100-year flood
   d. 130-30 fund

29. _____, anti-selection insurance, statistics, and risk management. It refers to a market process in which 'bad' results occur when buyers and sellers have asymmetric information (i.e. access to different information): the 'bad' products or customers are more likely to be selected. A bank that sets one price for all its checking account customers runs the risk of being adversely selected against by its low-balance, high-activity (and hence least profitable) customers.

   a. ACCRA Cost of Living Index
   b. Adverse selection
   c. AD-IA Model
   d. ACEA agreement

30. In economics, the _____ functional form of production functions is widely used to represent the relationship of an output to inputs. It was proposed by Knut Wicksell (1851-1926), and tested against statistical evidence by Charles Cobb and Paul Douglas in 1900-1928.

   For production, the function is

   $$Y = AL^{\alpha}K^{\beta},$$

   where:

   - Y = total production (the monetary value of all goods produced in a year)
   - L = labor input
   - K = capital input
   - A = total factor productivity
   - α and β are the output elasticities of labor and capital, respectively. These values are constants determined by available technology.

   Output elasticity measures the responsiveness of output to a change in levels of either labor or capital used in production, ceteris paribus. For example if $\alpha = 0.15$, a 1% increase in labor would lead to approximately a 0.15% increase in output.

a. Demand-pull theory
b. Growth accounting
c. Social savings
d. Cobb-Douglas

31. A _____ is a process of buying and selling goods when potential buyers submit their bids and potential sellers simultaneously submit their ask prices to an auctioneer, and then an auctioneer chooses some price p that clears the market: all the sellers who asked less than p sell and all buyers who bid more than p buy at this price p.

A _____ can be analyzed as a game. Players are buyers and sellers.

a. Repeated game
b. Complete information
c. Graph continuous
d. Double auction

32. _____ in economics and business is the result of an exchange and from that trade we assign a numerical monetary value to a good, service or asset. If Alice trades Bob 4 apples for an orange, the _____ of an orange is 4 apples. Inversely, the _____ of an apple is 1/4 oranges.

a. Price war
b. Premium pricing
c. Price book
d. Price

33. _____s are financial contracts whose values are derived from the value of something else (known as the underlying.) The underlying value on which a _____ is based can be an asset (e.g., commodities, equities (stocks), residential mortgages, commercial real estate, loans, bonds), an index (e.g., interest rates, exchange rates, stock market indices, consumer price index (CPI) -- see inflation _____s), weather conditions bonds or other forms of credit.

a. 100-year flood
b. Derivative
c. Second derivative
d. 130-30 fund

34. In finance, _____ is a measure of the sensitivity of the duration of a bond to changes in interest rates. There is an inverse relationship between _____ and sensitivity - in general, the higher the _____ less sensitive the bond price is to interest rate shifts, the lower the _____, the more sensitive it is.

Duration is a linear measure or 1st derivative of how the price of a bond changes in response to interest rate changes.

a. Russian financial crisis
b. Rule
c. Technocracy
d. Convexity

35. In mathematics, an _____ is a statement about the relative size or order of two objects, or about whether they are the same or not

- The notation a < b means that a is less than b.
- The notation a > b means that a is greater than b.
- The notation a ≠ b means that a is not equal to b, but does not say that one is greater than the other or even that they can be compared in size.

In each statement above, a is not equal to b. These relations are known as strict inequalities. The notation a < b may also be read as 'a is strictly less than b'.

Chapter 23. Incentives and Mechanism Design

a. Inequality
b. AD-IA Model
c. ACEA agreement
d. ACCRA Cost of Living Index

36. To _____ is to impose a financial charge or other levy upon a taxpayer by a state or the functional equivalent of a state.

_____es are also imposed by many subnational entities. _____es consist of direct _____ or indirect _____, and may be paid in money or as its labour equivalent (often but not always unpaid.)

a. 1921 recession
b. 100-year flood
c. Tax
d. 130-30 fund

37. To tax is to impose a financial charge or other levy upon a taxpayer by a state or the functional equivalent of a state.

_____ are also imposed by many subnational entities. _____ consist of direct tax or indirect tax, and may be paid in money or as its labour equivalent (often but not always unpaid.)

a. 130-30 fund
b. 1921 recession
c. Taxes
d. 100-year flood

38. _____ has several particular meanings:

- in mathematics
    - _____ function
    - Euler _____
    - _____
    - _____ subgroup
    - method of _____s (partial differential equations)
- in physics and engineering
    - any _____ curve that shows the relationship between certain input- and output parameters, e.g.
    - an I-V or current-voltage _____ is the current in a circuit as a function of the applied voltage
    - Receiver-Operator _____
- in fiction
    - in Dungeons ' Dragons, _____ is another name for ability score

a. Russian financial crisis
b. Technocracy
c. Characteristic
d. Demand

39. In linear algebra, a _____ is a square matrix in which the entries outside the main diagonal (â†") are all zero. The diagonal entries themselves may or may not be zero. Thus, the matrix D = ($d_{i,j}$) with n columns and n rows is diagonal if:

$$d_{i,j} = 0 \text{ if } i \neq j \quad \forall i, j \in \{1, 2, \ldots, n\}.$$

For example, the following matrix is diagonal:

$$\begin{bmatrix} 1 & 0 & 0 \\ 0 & 4 & 0 \\ 0 & 0 & -3 \end{bmatrix}.$$

The term _____ may sometimes refer to a rectangular _____, which is an m-by-n matrix with only the entries of the form $d_{i,i}$ possibly non-zero; for example,

$$\begin{bmatrix} 1 & 0 & 0 \\ 0 & 4 & 0 \\ 0 & 0 & -3 \\ 0 & 0 & 0 \end{bmatrix}, \text{ or}$$

a. Transpose
c. Diagonal matrix
b. 130-30 fund
d. 100-year flood

40. In microeconomics, _____ is quite simply the conversion of inputs into outputs. It is an economic process that uses resources to create a good or service that is suitable for exchange. This can include manufacturing, storing, shipping, and packaging.
a. Solved
c. MET
b. Production
d. Red Guards

Chapter 1
1. d   2. a   3. b   4. d   5. a   6. d   7. c

Chapter 2
1. a   2. d   3. c   4. d   5. b   6. a   7. d   8. c   9. a   10. c
11. d   12. a   13. d   14. d   15. b   16. a   17. d   18. a   19. a

Chapter 3
1. a   2. b   3. d   4. d   5. d   6. d   7. a   8. a   9. d   10. d
11. a   12. d   13. c   14. b   15. b   16. b   17. c   18. c   19. d   20. d
21. d   22. c   23. d   24. d   25. d   26. d   27. a   28. d   29. d   30. b
31. d

Chapter 4
1. a   2. d   3. d   4. d   5. d   6. d   7. b   8. a   9. d   10. d
11. d   12. b   13. c

Chapter 5
1. a   2. c   3. c   4. c   5. c   6. d   7. c   8. d   9. d   10. c
11. d   12. d   13. d   14. d   15. b   16. c   17. b   18. d   19. d   20. a
21. d   22. c   23. d   24. a   25. d

Chapter 6
1. d   2. a   3. d   4. d   5. d   6. d   7. a   8. d   9. a   10. b
11. d   12. a   13. a   14. b   15. d   16. b   17. c   18. d   19. b   20. a
21. b   22. d   23. b   24. d

Chapter 7
1. c   2. c   3. d   4. d   5. d   6. d   7. d   8. b   9. a   10. c
11. a

Chapter 8
1. d   2. a   3. d   4. d   5. b   6. b   7. d   8. d   9. d   10. d
11. d   12. d   13. d   14. b   15. b   16. b

Chapter 9
1. d   2. a   3. b   4. a   5. b   6. d   7. d   8. d   9. b   10. d
11. d   12. c   13. d   14. b   15. a   16. c   17. a   18. b   19. d

Chapter 10
1. c   2. c   3. c   4. d   5. c   6. d   7. d   8. b   9. c   10. d
11. d   12. d   13. c   14. d   15. d   16. d   17. d   18. b   19. b   20. d
21. d   22. d   23. b   24. b   25. c   26. a   27. d   28. d   29. d   30. b
31. a   32. d   33. a   34. a   35. d   36. d   37. c   38. b   39. b   40. a
41. b   42. d

ANSWER KEY

Chapter 11
1. d   2. b   3. a   4. b   5. d   6. d   7. b   8. c   9. d   10. d
11. b   12. b   13. d   14. d   15. a   16. a   17. d   18. d   19. d   20. c
21. d   22. d   23. c   24. c   25. d

Chapter 12
1. b   2. d   3. a   4. d   5. a   6. d   7. d   8. d   9. a   10. d
11. c   12. a   13. d   14. d   15. a   16. d   17. c   18. d   19. a   20. c
21. b   22. d   23. d   24. c   25. d   26. b   27. a   28. a   29. b   30. d
31. c   32. a   33. d   34. a   35. d   36. d   37. d   38. c

Chapter 13
1. d   2. d   3. c   4. c   5. a   6. c   7. d   8. d   9. d   10. a
11. c   12. d   13. d   14. d   15. a   16. d   17. d   18. c   19. c   20. d
21. d   22. c

Chapter 14
1. d   2. b   3. b   4. d   5. a   6. d   7. d   8. d   9. a   10. d
11. a   12. d   13. a   14. d   15. d

Chapter 15
1. d   2. a   3. c   4. a   5. c   6. c   7. b   8. d   9. c   10. a
11. d   12. d   13. d   14. a   15. a   16. d   17. a   18. d   19. d   20. d
21. a   22. b   23. d   24. b   25. b   26. d   27. a   28. b   29. a   30. d
31. a   32. a   33. d   34. d

Chapter 16
1. c   2. c   3. a   4. a   5. c   6. d   7. c   8. d   9. d   10. b
11. a   12. a   13. a   14. a   15. d   16. c   17. a   18. b   19. c   20. d
21. c   22. a   23. d   24. d   25. a   26. d   27. c   28. b   29. c   30. a
31. d   32. a   33. c   34. d   35. c   36. b   37. d

Chapter 17
1. c   2. c   3. d   4. d   5. d   6. d   7. b   8. d   9. a   10. a
11. d   12. d   13. d   14. b   15. b   16. c   17. c   18. d   19. d   20. b
21. c   22. c   23. d   24. b   25. d   26. d   27. a   28. a   29. d

Chapter 18
1. d   2. d   3. c   4. d   5. b   6. d   7. d   8. d   9. d   10. c
11. d   12. d   13. d   14. a   15. d   16. d   17. a   18. c   19. b   20. a
21. a   22. d   23. d   24. b   25. d

Chapter 19
1. c	2. d	3. d	4. b	5. d	6. a	7. d	8. d	9. a	10. d
11. b	12. c	13. d	14. a	15. d	16. d	17. d	18. d	19. c	20. a
21. d	22. d	23. d	24. b	25. d	26. c	27. a	28. b	29. a	30. b
31. d	32. c	33. d	34. b	35. d	36. d				

Chapter 20
1. a	2. c	3. d	4. b	5. d	6. d	7. d	8. d	9. d	10. a
11. d	12. a	13. d	14. d	15. d	16. d	17. a	18. a	19. b	20. d
21. d	22. a	23. b	24. b	25. d	26. b	27. c	28. d	29. a	30. d
31. d	32. d	33. d	34. d	35. d	36. b	37. d	38. d	39. a	

Chapter 21
1. c	2. a	3. b	4. c	5. d	6. a	7. d	8. c	9. d	10. d

Chapter 22
1. d	2. d	3. d	4. c	5. d	6. b	7. d	8. d	9. d	10. d
11. d	12. d	13. c	14. c	15. d	16. c	17. b	18. a	19. a	20. d
21. b									

Chapter 23
1. d	2. d	3. d	4. d	5. c	6. c	7. a	8. d	9. a	10. a
11. a	12. d	13. a	14. d	15. b	16. a	17. d	18. d	19. a	20. d
21. d	22. a	23. d	24. d	25. b	26. c	27. d	28. a	29. b	30. d
31. d	32. d	33. b	34. d	35. a	36. c	37. c	38. c	39. c	40. b

www.ingramcontent.com/pod-product-compliance
Lightning Source LLC
Chambersburg PA
CBHW082040230426
43670CB00016B/2724